WHAT DECIDED
CHRISTIANITY

Event and Experience in the New Testament

Cover picture:
'Steps towards Gethsemane
from the Hill of Zion as
trodden in the Gospel.'
(Author's photograph)

'The love of Christ makes up our mind.'

Saint Paul: *2. Corinthians 5.14*

'What lacks then of perfection fit for God
But just the instance which this tale supplies
Of love without a limit? So is strength,
So is intelligence: let love be so,
Unlimited in its self-sacrifice.
Then is the tale true and God shows complete.'

Robert Browning:
The Ring and the Book, X. 1367-72.

'I, too, followed Him,
Married my frailty to His virtue, and
Helped Him reveal Himself . . .'

Tawfiq Sayigh, Palestinian Poet.
The Sermon on the Mount.

'We have known and believed the Love God has to us.'

Saint John. His *First Epistle. 4.16*

'Fidei coticula Crux.'
'The original site of Christianity is the fact of Christ.'

P. Carnegie Simpson.

'You would know your Lord's meaning in this thing? Know it
well. Love was His meaning. Who showed it to you? Love. What
did He show you? Love. Why did He show it? For love. Hold on
to this and you will know and understand.'

Julian of Norwich:
Revelations of Divine Love. Chap LXXXVI.

What Decided Christianity

Event and Experience in the New Testament

KENNETH CRAGG

CHURCHMAN PUBLISHING
1989

What Decided Christianity
by
Kenneth Cragg
was first published in 1989 by
Churchman Publishing Limited
117 Broomfield Avenue
Worthing, West Sussex BN14 7SF

Publisher: Peter Smith

Copyright © Kenneth Cragg 1989

Represented in
Dublin; Sydney; Wellington;
Kingston, Ontario and Wilton, Connecticut

Distributed to the book trade by
Bailey Book Distribution Limited
(a division of the Bailey and Swinfen Holdings Group)
Warner House, Wear Bay Road
Folkestone, Kent CT19 6PH

ISBN 1 85093,113 5

*Printed in Great Britain by
John Penry Press, Swansea*

Contents

Other books by Kenneth Cragg:

The Call of the Minaret, New edition, Collins, 1985.

The Christ and the Faiths, S.P.C.K., 1986.

Muhammad and the Christian, Darton, Longman & Todd, 1982.

Jesus and the Muslim, Allen & Unwin, 1985.

Poetry of the Word, Churchman, 1987.

The Pen and the Faith: Eight Muslim Writers and the Qur'ān, Allen & Unwin, 1985.

Readings in the Qur'ān, Collins, 1988.

Preface

The word 'Christianity' comes from the word 'Christ' but only by way of 'Christian.' Otherwise we would have Christism, on the pattern of 'Buddhism' or 'Hinduism.' Three nouns in one, moving from the first to the third only through the second, 'Christ' goes into 'Christian' and 'Christian' into 'Christianity.'

It may seem trite to start with something so obvious. But the point captures a large theme this book aims to explore. Christianity derives from event and experience and its defining document, the New Testament, exists only through both in their inter-action. Being Christian arises from a decision of faith through which and in which the Christ whom it received came himself to be, historically and credally, the Christ he was. An experience of discovery and acknowledgement belonged inseparably with an event of disclosure and grace. The event, by its very nature, turned on the recognition. The realisation knew and greeted what the event made real. The Christ was the theme and love of the Christian only because the Christian was the text of the Christ.

When, in 1970, Professor C.H. Dodd, a noted New Testament scholar, published *The Founder of Christianity* there were other scholars who queried the title as dubious, or even tendentious. Had Jesus ever intended the Church? Had Christianity any founder? If so, was it not Paul? Was it feasible at all to speak of 'Christianity' as any one thing? The questions multiply. Some will occupy us later.

Yet Charles Dodd's title was appropriate but only if we may think of Jesus as 'the found of Christianity' with 'Christians' as the finders. Being the Christ, or as the Hebrew word is, *Mashiah*, entailed credentials. These in no way derived from their acceptance, as if the faith had fathered itself. They brought their own disconcerting claim and quality. It was in acceptance that they were discerned and, through discernment, found their living proof. Identity is at once

7

something possessed and something known — not one without the other. What Jesus was in Messianic achievement he was known to be in the conviction of the disciples.

Christianity, then, is rightly so named as the 'event' of Jesus as the Christ and the 'experience' that made Christians. The genesis of the faith was the movement of fact into conviction, of conviction responsive to fact. What Jesus was to his disciples was only accomplished in what he moved his disciples to become to him. If he was the 'founder' of Christianity it lay in their being found by him in the founding, as the Christ whom their souls loved.

This reciprocal situation between Christ-event and Christian experience the chapters here mean to examine from the several angles of their New Testament portrayal. They have to do with narrative and nurture, with meaning and ministry, with sacrament and soul. There are a variety of reasons why such examination is urgent. New Testament scholarship is rightly meticulous and necessarily professional. But for decades now it has tended to pre-occupy itself with bewildering minutiae liable to dismay the uninitiated searching for the authentic content. There are some writers who conclude with inconclusive scepticisms through unwillingness or failure to reckon with how and why the New Testament exists at all. The great Albert Schweitzer, in 1906, in *The Quest of the Historical Jesus* captured the agenda in a now famous title. In a memorable concluding passage he wrote of himself and his contemporaries as coming to Jesus 'as to one unknown.' In doubt of the first century they would 'know him' in the 20th 'in the toils, the conflicts, the sufferings' they would 'pass through in his fellowship and . . . in their own experience' learn who he is. In that moving call to discipleship, despite the puzzle of the 'historical quest,' is it strange to ask why he, and we, may not get beyond 'one unknown' by means of the very literature — the New Testament itself — in which the original disciples learned and told who he had proved to be in their immediate 'experience' of his 'fellowship.'?

Popularists, without Schweitzer's deep reverence, have clouded and confused the issues, with their 'Passover plots' and non-existent Jesuses, trivialising as they did so. Others stay only with what they list as the 'unanswered questions' as if the New Testament, in itself, were not the inclusive 'answer' within which alone 'questions' exist. For the interrogatives with which — wisely or unwisely — we dissect and speculate and query belong only by grace of a great affirmative and the literature that made it.

Exploring 'What Decided Christianity' (the title is *not* a question) is vital for the further reason that the meeting of religions is increasingly a right and urgent feature of our time. The concept, and the practice, of inter-faith relations enter intimately into both theology and society today. It is, therefore, well that Christian participation should be articulate and eager, ready to bring its distinctive dimension to all mutual engagement. The chapters here were complete before the appearance of the recent symposium: *The Myth of Christian Uniqueness,* and thus did not have it in mind. The writers use the word 'myth' in a mischievous ambiguity, intending a frame of reference but suggesting a fallacy. 'Uniqueness' has never been a Christian term and does not exist in the New Testament. For it excludes all over-lap of meaning and experience between faith-concerns. To do so is manifestly false. But 'distinctive' — welcoming such over-lap — is right and important. There *is* that about Christianity which is *not* found elsewhere in the same harmony, and hopefulness. It is that inclusive quality which is captured in the credal, scriptural language about 'the only begotten Son,' understanding 'only' and 'begotten' in the sense of a divine self-disclosure implemented from within the divine nature with a wholeness and a fulness (what the New Testament called the *pleroma)* which due reverence for the divine mystery need not, and does not, distrust as being somehow either partial or elusive. If we are truly to relate that distinctive quality of 'God in Christ' to an open heart for other believers and unbeliefs we need to know and hold it as it truly is.

But the Christian Scripture is rich in metaphor and imagery often remote from present consciousness. It involves a confidence in the very nature of language which has sadly seeped away from current mentality in the West, distrustful or scornful of all but the 'provens' of the test-tube, the computer and the market-place. Prevailing empiricism shapes

an unwelcome climate for the instinctive sense of wonder
and of awe that belong with the verdict for faith. How does
'blood cleanse' when in fact it only stains? What meaning can
attach to 'God and the Lamb.'? Or who — without the elusive
clue — can intelligently sing:

> 'Fruit of the mystic rose, as of that rose the stem,
> The root whence mercy ever flows, the babe of Bethlehem'?

People are embarrassingly ill at ease with such strange and
'mystic' language, mixing its metaphors and disconcerting
all but its music. Must it not be consigned to the idle
fancies of the self deluded?

A faith that is, for present communication, so far
encumbered by its vocabulary and its traditions has a heavy
task in capturing an alien audience for the truth within them.
Distractions are rampant anyway and 'lending of the ears'
is hard to gain and keep. The more reason, then, for
striving to ensure that if Christianity is to be ignored it will
not be for lack of knowing what is truly was and how it came
to be. There is vital need to have it in terms of the natal
decision in which it first consisted and in which it still avails.

Such study is urgent in another way within the churches.
Postures which claim for themselves absolute possession of
the Christian identity should not forget the quality of event
and experience, of dynamic decision, in which it had its
genesis. Only there have they any ground at all. Whether
named Biblical, Orthodox, Catholic, Reformed, Evangelical,
or otherwise, they all derive from origins too vital, too crucial,
for the overtones these names have since acquired. It is
important to find anew the Christ-into-Christian-into-
Christianity experience as it truly was, if we are to free it
from the pride of heritage or the lust for guarantee to which
institutionalising is always prone.

Though the faith, as Jude had it, is 'once for all delivered
to the saints,' that trust is no deposit in a bank. The security
which forms and formularies and authority purport to
offer stands, not in them, but in the living experience. All
absolutes whether of dogma or of form have to justify the
warrant by which they claim to be so. With the submission
piety brings to them there has always to be the question why

it did so. That question has to remain for ever open — most of all so where we like to think it closed. Some religious minds yearn for the repose of finality and go to great lengths to locate it beyond the proper anxieties of a right integrity. It is just such anxieties which active faith embraces in sustained decision. Hence this study now of what the Christian decision historically was, as far as history can impart it to us.

If the reader finds allusions from one chapter to another that is only because of the unity of the theme.

Attempting so rich a whole in so terse a form it seems wise to forego the luxury of footnotes and a prolixity of verse references. A broad canvas and a few bold strokes must risk the absence of minute detail. Those familiar with the New Testament will know where to look and the select Bibliography may serve others. It is the heart, not the incidentals, of what must obtain between scholarship and faith which pre-occupies us here. We can better read in the margins when we have realised the theme inside them.

Some will see the enterprise as imprudent, even fool-hardy. That 'first, fine, careless rapture' is two millenia away. Others will fear that, even if we could be sure of its reality then, the centuries — or at least our own — have withdrawn it, like an obsolete language, from our options. Yet options with minds and wills to take them refuse to be outdated. The first identity of Christianity is emphatically among them. There are those who decide that 'unanswered questions', and the integrity which stays with them, are more precious and authentic than the way of commitment and discipleship. To each their option.

Either way, there is a will to believe or a will to disbelieve. It is finally on the will that the issue in these chapters turns. Freely staked, as it is, in personal decision its dependable credentials are in Jesus as the Christ. The New Testament, both as life and literature, is 'the tribute of the current to that source.' To realise the whence and the whither of that current is to live as 'Christian' in its thrust and fulness. It is to receive within oneself the impulse of that 'love of God which is in Christ Jesus our Lord.' Be sure that, through all the chapters with their 'Christ' dimensions we are 'having to do with God. It is precisely in being about Jesus that this is a book about God.

Oxford, 1988.   *Kenneth Cragg*

Introduction

There can be no honest doubt that Christianity was initiated in a drama of decision which amazed those who made it and in the making revolutionised their sense of God. 'The love of Christ decides us' was their personal and corporate verdict on themselves and all the issues of their world. They meant the love of Christ received and recognised in the whole dimension of theology, returned and ratified by love for Christ in the whole design of life. This faith, with its inherent creation of community, these pages aim to sift and understand in order to discover the distinctive heart of Christianity. Our concern is with the finding of those convictions about God and humanity through which the finders found themselves and received the name of 'Christians.'

The quality of that inaugurating decision, entailed upon them by the events of Jesus, and translated into their openness to the world, has been often obscured by the minutiae of New Testament study. Few fields of historical enquiry have been more quarried and searched than those of Christian origins. Few are more liable to tendentious treatment, thanks to the vested interests which establishments, academic and religious, are apt to generate. Attention to minutiae is necessary in its place. Exemption from their claims and tedium is not sought here. But they should not be allowed to distract or divert the mind from the central reality within the Christian Scripture and the faith which wrote it. The distinctive conviction about God as active love must dominate all else, with its corollary of a humanity inclusively within an undifferentiating activity of grace.

Those who reached and held it did so from within the significance of Jesus. They discerned it in the fabric of his living as 'the Son of the Father.' It was confirmed to them in the self-giving of his ministry and the climax of the Cross and the Resurrection. These, in their whole meaning, the Christian decision identified as the Messianic fact, the

13

disconcerting but conclusive realisation of the ancient hope. Messiah being in Hebraic terms the agent of the divine sovereignty, Christian love and logic made bold to identify Messiah Jesus with the very character of God. They concluded that this Messiahship should be read as the index to the divine nature. The love of the Christ — in Jesus — made up their minds about the eternal matrix of the divine initiative long awaited and veritably fulfilled.

In Jesus as 'the Word made flesh' they read — as the Greek of John 1.18 has it — the very 'exegesis of God.' They reached the confidence that what had transpired from Jesus' birth to his ascension, from Nazareth through Gethsemane to Easter, had 'expounded' God in an inclusive historical sacrament of truth through personality. In him they came, as they believed, into 'the knowledge and the love of God,' in event and in experience. Their confession and initial creed was simply: 'Our Lord Jesus Christ . . .' — the sum of their discovery and the ground of their fellowship. They learned to recognise the kingdom of heaven in the wounds of Jesus and knew it open to all.

This central focus must discipline all related issues of due scholarly concern for Christian integrity. It must also control a Christian presence in the converse of faiths today when the inter-action of religions is so much on the agenda — and *loquenda*. The call to dialogue is familiar enough. Its very frequency tends to make for a too facile temper and its pursuit may be too sanguine. We need depth and honesty both in what we find and in what we bring, lest dialogue become complacent. The very urgency of co-existence requires us to explore its implications intelligently and with a right frankness.

It is not the manner of inter-religious meeting which is in question, except in diehard quarters, but the content. Habits of suspicion and attitudes of indifference or denigration are to be repudiated. We must do amicably and to our utmost all that can be done in common. Majority faiths have to respond generously and effectively to the demands made upon their social and legal institutions by the needs and aspirations of minority groups. The idea of pluralism has to find its way into our traditional assumptions to stimulate the necessary adjustment in the set of minds and the patterns of culture. Religion, we have to acknowledge, cannot well be contemporary unless it be inter-religious in awareness and temper. Central to the integrity of any faith must be its readiness for the presence of others.

These counsels are amply argued and commended in numerous popular manuals and studies. But, precisely because things are so, it is the more urgent that the content of our mental engagement with each other should be articulate and adequate. We need also to be sufficiently aware of the danger present in easy language about pluralism in society. Multiform culture is liable to be a dubious concept, if not also a contradiction in terms. For the things which constitute human identity — whatsoever identity it be — are so bonded in birth, history, geography, law, time and place, as to be capable of conceding pluralism only by patient and discerning response, never by negligence or bland sentiment. It is here that historic faiths have so keen a test of their resilience under the constraints and in the confusions of co-existence. The inter-play of identity and hospitality is a precarious thing. The more ecumenical in our sympathies and range we mean to be the more appropriate an authentic custody of the faith which informs our intention.

The case itself for tolerance can, and does at times, dissolve into vacuity and mental sloth. Nor can tolerance pretend to be value-free. Even minimally it must be against intolerance of which religions have been, and remain, criminally capable. Intolerance of intolerance pre-supposes meanings urgent for affirmation and not to be neutralised in supine unanimity or seduced into prostitution. The capacity to disagree may thus be a sound ingredient of genuine converse. For faiths are not reducible to genial compatibles. Certainly Buddhism is not, nor Islam, nor Judaism, nor Christianity. It is right, therefore, that the decision which made Christianity at the outset should inform and determine its presence now in all its range and quality within the inter-religious scene.

The fond imagery sometimes proposed in inter-faith discussion can easily betray, or simply ignore, this decisiveness. One of the most familiar of such analogies tells of a mountain being scaled from different sides, preferably in misty conditions, by a variety of climbers unbeknown to one another. They are ascending, nevertheless, albeit deviously, to the same summit. Such imagery misses the radical disparities existing between faiths as to the mountain itself, the penetrating of the mist, the capacity of the climbers and the goal they intend in their summitry.

Further, the appeal to mystery on which such concepts depend is itself as much in debate, as liable for its credentials, as the doctrines or codes or cults it is employed to reproach and assumed to transcend.

First to blindfold men, set them to identify some parabolic elephant and have them pronounce differently about its various items of anatomy, trunk, tail and flank, is hardly an intelligent portrayal of what transpires when Buddhist meets Muslim or Jew the Christian.

The meeting of religions, however, is not here our theme, but rather the Christian dimension to be brought to it in true openness. That Christianity is a faith with a far-reaching debt to Judaism and a lively conversation with Hinduism, Buddhism and Islam is a matter for glad recognition. But it does not alter the fact that the Christian holds a faith-reality which stands in sharp distinction from all else. The heart of this distinctiveness the chapters here aim to take into reckoning both historically and doctrinally. They do so, not in any spiritual or intellectual dis-engagement with all else, but as the necessary discipline of real engagement.

The first chapter sets down the crucial happening which gave Christian faith its birth and created Christian community. As is always the case with significant history what happened was a fusion of event and experience. Factuality stood — and stands — in these together, in mutual confirmation. Event did not happen in the absence of meaning comprehending it, nor did experience eventuate apart from a taking place. The narrative and the conviction of the New Testament inter-depend in this way. We would have neither without the other. Our first duty in respect of the Gospels is to appreciate this situation, for it determines their character. The documentation they present is witness, neither chronicling what is extraneous to experience, nor contriving what is suggested by imagination, but confessing a faith *via* the significance of a history.

Equally the Letters of the New Testament exemplify this distilling of event into experience. Prior, for the most part, to the Gospels when these had their final shape, the Epistles give access to the context of the steady process within which the forming and composing of the Gospels ensued. Both were emerging in the third quarter of the first Christian century. But what they came to embody in its dramatic essentials had been resolved three decades earlier in the wake of the living incidence of Jesus at the turn of the twenties and thirties of the century. As the historian, Herbert Butterfield observes:

> 'The Christian religion, based on belief in the risen Christ emerged . . . with a rapidity which must be staggering to any historian . . . Some sudden illumination enabled them (the disciples) to fit everything into place . . . in the years and, indeed, in the weeks . . .'

Our first obligation is to have the measure of that drama of event-experience in this intense focus of realisation, the event-experience of the Christ as Jesus, of Jesus as the Christ, the theme of faith and the faith that grasped its theme.

Chapter 2 turns from that sense of dramatic decision to its long antecedents in Messianic hope. Through all its vicissitudes this hope reached back into the entire Biblical perspective of creation and of humanity under God. Given these, it belonged instinctively with Israel in covenant. How disparate, how sharply contentious, were Messianic expectations in the time of Jesus is evident from his own story. Kingship, priesthood, Torah-community, revolt, competed for their meaning and fulfilment in Messianic terms. The questions: Who? and How? and When? and Where? about Messiah troubled anxious piety and vexed the public scene.

It was this theme and all its ambiguities which underlay both the puzzle and the clue in Jesus' ministry. If there is enigma in the story its resolution is here. The Gospels may leave us unsure about how to trace and formulate the Messianic consciousness of Jesus but they leave us in no doubt whatever about his Messianic achievement. They say that Jesus ended all ambiguity in the long yearning for Messiah by who and how he was in life and death. He had

done so in the meaning of his Sonship to the Father through
the obedience of a love that suffered. These are the very heart
of the New Testament decision about him. The Messianic
purpose and the Messianic person had come together. Men
knew who he was in seeing how he was. These together were
the catalyst determining the faith of the Church, the
making of its corporate mind on account of the mind of Jesus
as the Christ.

In turn the Christian Scriptures became the documentation of education in his mind proceeding in the cherishing
of recollection and the discovery of vocation. They lived by
the sense that Jesus had translated into history the very mind
of God. He had done so in a Messiahship moving through
the Sermon on the Mount to the travail of Gethsemane and
the climax of resurrection. The disciples became apostles —
there is a significant progression in the terms — in believing the fulfilled Messiahship according to Jesus to be the
very credentials by which to decide about God. There we,
in our turn, read and comprehend a Christ-shaped story. This
is the task of chapter 2.

This comprehension leads in chapter 3 to the Christ-telling
faith. As the key to Christianity the decision we are studying was necessarily cumulative. As with great art, so with
living faith, responsiveness is the vital factor in its meaning.
'That which knitteth souls and prospers love' brings a new
perception in which to understand and interpret the world.
In the New Testament there came a new range and warmth
of theology and a thrust of fellowship extending beyond its
Jewish origins into the open world and, so doing, incurring
the encounters and questions of that wider space and longer
time.

Conviction is firmly anchored within its Palestinian locale
and 'the days of Jesus' there. But it moves into other
birthrights of human kind, now perceived to have them.
Inaugural generations, no less than others, live with the
receding horizon of the future. The trauma of the Fall of
Jerusalem in A.D. 70 required the Church to revise its sense
of time to come. In our reckoning with the New Testament
we have to appreciate these exigencies of an expanding and
suffering people. The text which has to do with Jesus

historically has the subtext of a Jesus possessed in the vicissitudes of communities 'gathered in his name.' That scattered fellowship is united in the image of the remembered Christ and with the mandate of witness tests and tells its theme. Its mission and its theology define each other.

They also prescribe character. Christ-dwelling life, we may say, belongs in Christ-telling faith. The pastoral nurture of apostolic communities is in the loved idiom of the historical retrospect to Galilee and the Cross. Being and conduct consist in believing, *Confessio fidei* means *imitatio Christi.* The story of Jesus in his history is told as a summons into his example. Continually the mind of Christ in his deeds is enjoined on readers in the Epistles as also to be theirs. 'Let this mind be in you that was in him,' 'Arm yourselves with the same mind' — these are the rubrics of behaviour. Record and recollection and regime are one. The ethics of the Gospel are infused into the self-reckoning of the discipleship. 'The meekness and gentleness of Christ' are cited in a phrase that has the feel of common currency familiar to all.

The New Testament is thus the literature of new community. It has as much to do with what we are to become, and why, as with what we can believe. Either way, its concern is the expression of Christ. Nor is this Christ-dwelling only a mentality informing character. It embraces the art of worship. Implicit liturgy lies within the New Testament in company with explicit ethics. There are traces, as in the great passage in Philippians 2.5-11, of early Christian hymns celebrating the themes of faith. The theology elaborating the Jesus history moves with adoration of God. For perceptive mind is only authentic in the wonder of the soul. The music of conviction is the chorus of doxology. 'The throne of God and of the Lamb' is paradox in praise.

It is noteworthy in this sense how both Gospels and Epistles draw a clear analogy between Jesus and the Temple at Jerusalem. 'The place of the Name,' in the old idiom, that rendezvous where God was to be named and known, has become the point of the personality. Christians are 'in Christ' whether they be 'at Philippi,' 'at Corinth' or where-ever they sojourn. The sacred locale is where Christ's presence synchronises with 'two or three met together in his name.'

This temple-role of Jesus belongs with the other meaning of 'the temple of his body.' Faith in the Incarnation means that 'every place is hallowed ground.'

It will be clear through all the foregoing in chapters 1 to 5 that we are involved in issues we did not stay to broach while we were concentrating on what decided Christianity. We have to take up in all frankness the many queries, caveats and contrary verdicts which are urged against any such decision. Popular impressionists and erudite scholars, not to say partisans, dispute and disavow the case we have made. They offer a diversity of argument against the very notion of any positive conviction effectively identifying Christianity, whether initially within the New Testament or credibly in the long centuries since. These disavowals with the bewilderments they generate have to be patiently faced on their merits.

But doing so at least involves some decisive case from which to begin. There is only confusion and futility in a proliferation of debate which has not stayed to reckon with the implications of the actual sequel to Jesus occurring in the New Testament *per se,* the tribute of the current to the source. There may well be details of conjecture or obscurity but these cannot well be weighed or accommodated as such, in the absence of perspective of the whole. That is a pseudo-scholarship for which the margins matter more than the text or the sum is lost in mistaking the equation. If we are to escape partiality we must be concerned with a whole.

Indeed, it is only by refusing partial attitudes that we begin to wrestle with the things at stake in New Testament history and interpretation as they really are. They involve the Messianic meaning itself and whether Jesus reliably belonged with it and the consciousness in which he could have done so. There is, further, the relation between the mind of Jesus and the mind of the Church. There are tensions between the historian and the theologian in the use of the Gospels and the true connection between the faith of Jesus and the faith about him. Were there unwarranted factors in the growth of Christology? Must we suspect Greek or pagan influences muddying Hebraic concepts? What of the origins of new community in Christ, its tense relations within and alongside Judaism and how such tensions conditioned the written presentation of Jesus, especially in John's Gospel? Through all these runs the vexed, and vexing, issue of authority within Christian ministry, the very propriety — or perversity — of Churchness itself. All these, and not least, the last, beset the minds not only of external researchers and pundits but of Christian interpreters in interior controversy. Can Christianity in any way be thought of as decisive at all?

There are still more daunting sources of dissent from Christian identity as finally discernible or desirable. Down all the centuries are grievous compromises of Christian history itself — polemic, schism, excommunication, and the crimes of Byzantium and Rome and many a lesser centre. There is all the tawdry, tortuous, tainted story of Christian existence. In face of all, is it not futile to pretend or affirm some pure, credible, durable decision by which Christianity could be identified and wanted? Is it not as capable as any other faith of wild assurance, vulgar prejudice, irrational excess, tepid formalism and downright villainy? Is not its record stained by demonic manifestations of pride and myriad grievings of the Holy Spirit? Are we not arguably left with a cynic's choice between admiring a Christianity that never long existed or regretting the one that did exist too long? And what, today, of its seemingly incongruous arrival into a secular atrophy precisely where its writ was most surely thought to run?

Hence the necessity of a chapter concerning 'questions ever present.' Chapter 6 could well be longer than all the rest together. That, were it so, would still not make the book lopsided. Statement of decision may well be briefer than its vindication. And, faced as they must duly be, these immense dissuasives strangely corroborate the very category of decision for which we are concerned. A Christian faith, despite them, is an option for which we decide, an interpretation on which we resolve.

Faith, by its very nature does not, and cannot, have the absoluteness that belongs, for example, to mathematics. Could it do so it would not be religious. If we are saying: 'Amen' to the New Testament and therein to Christ it is both a 'Verily it is so,' *and* 'Let it be thus.' The credentials are there,

full, free, open and reliable but not infallible. Faith is the
verdict which takes and salutes their quality in a readiness
to proceed upon them. To be so ready does not first require
a banning of all contrary options of mind or will, the
arguable dissent disowning it in others.

The poet Browning's challenge:
> 'Like you this Christianity, or No?
> Has it your vote to be so if it can?'

fits his robust mood, if not, perhaps the wisest metaphor
to make the point. Faith was never rightly warranted by some
closing of the mind or numbing of the soul. No intelligent
approach to the New Testament proceeds upon categories
that ignore the nature of its own genesis, the implications
of its own form and character. It is not like some telephone
directory where enquiry is that of mere number and
in-errancy — misprints apart. Numbers house no issues in
their dreary columns. One does not have to engage with such
authority, undertake the puzzle of motives in the making or
ponder literary process in its shape. Not so the Gospels and
Epistles. They did not originate nor can they be read in
vacuum of mind. Their precious cargo of record about Jesus,
of his comprehended significance, was first entrusted to
fallible spirits in the working world. It was risked in the
jeopardy of receding years and changing scenes. There was
hiatus, reflection, composition, between their initiation in
logia, homily, and hymn, and their final quality as text and
literature. Given these vital, and precarious, processes of
formation, of editorialia and proximate currency, it is clear
that nothing infallibilist, dispensing with scholarship or
disowning enquiry, can properly attach to faith about them.

We are back to decision. Christian revelation in the
meaning of the Incarnation, and in the consequent fabric
of the New Testament portrayal, is of the sort to await what
it requires. It expects a perceptive, sifting, responsive faith,
tuned to its own idiom in the actual Jesus and a growing,
struggling Church. There were, and are, hazards all along
the way. That the decision of faith is, therefore, open to
challenge, summoned to show reason, liable to be suspect,
and so always on its mettle, is precisely the situation it
presupposes in the trust of its witness.

This, however, does not mean that it is a faith standing only in its own assertion, as if it were a faith in faith. It does not imply that the preaching in itself constitutes the Gospel, all historical reference apart. This is to make the *kerugma* all there was. Faith does not substantiate itself oblivious of the status of its own content. Nor are status and content to be explained as the projection into suppositious objectivity of some wistful subjectivity of humanity, giving pseudo (if consolatory) existence to that with which nothing real corresponds.

To equate the decision within Christian faith as a 'thinking makes it so' is not to reckon either with its history or its content. It is not 'thinking that makes it so' but — in total contrast — a thinking of what is so, a decision consisting in response to divine self-disclosure recognised and loved. It is, no doubt, open to the sceptic to say that this sense of responding does not escape the charge of delusion but merely gives delusion a falsely re-assuring form, the whole conviction being, in fact, self-generating. That is the sceptic's option. There is no criterion to adjudicate between the believer's conviction about faith as response and the sceptic's insistence that it has no ground but itself. Could faith expect it to be otherwise?

The suspicion, or accusation, about mere 'faith in faith' thus brings us around again to the reality of decision. To hold that response to revelation *is* response — and not projection — is not something that response can 'prove'. Response can only point to the actuality which kindled and grounded that conviction. Nor can revelation command some extraneous credential external to its capacity in kindling and warranting such response. Neither revelation nor faith can be attested outside their own recognizances with and in each other. Cynic and sceptic may resolve to accede to neither. That option of theirs, merely by being unhappily taken, does not disqualify the mortise and tenon pattern joining faith to meaning. In Christian decision they came, and come, together in Jesus as the Christ and in the acknowledgement by Christian faith of that divine self-disclosure.

Of all the questions ever present that of God is always the

first and the last. 'Him with whom we have to do' is the
Bible way of defining where faith responds, with Jesus as 'the
author and finisher,' the 'architect and pioneer' of such faith.
But all awaits and intends a human acknowledgement — a
situation which, in its generous uncompulsiveness and open
risk, is a silent, eloquent intimation of who and how God
is. 'He who comes to God,' says the New Testament, 'must
believe that He is.' For Christians in original definition, who
He is meant who He was seen to be, to have been, and ever
willed to be, in Jesus, in word and deed and wounds 'God
manifest.'

The story of that Christian acknowledgement of God in
Christ is the birth narrative of Christianity. By those terms
and that temper of its origin, it is a faith called to live always
in self-interrogation as to its credentials as the only right
condition of their commendation to the world. To stand by
what decided Christianity is to take those credentials into
an open future.

What, then, of the perennial decision now? The issues of
integrity and scholarship which we have had in mind in
chapter 6 are only part of what an intelligent faith must
undertake today. As many have been known to murmur to
themselves, listening to some modern day evangelist
preaching the Cross: 'All that is a long time ago.' It is as John
Bunyan graphically had it with his Evangelist pointing his
burdened Pilgrim, hand stretched 'over a very wide field,'
to a dimly deciphered 'wicket gate.' A very wide field indeed
distances us from the decision of the first Christians. Can
it be appropriate still to identify in a single history the focal
point of all history? Or to acknowledge in a single cross the
inclusive open secret of what evil means and how grace saves,
'Christ crucified veritably the power and wisdom of God.'?
It is a faith which has always been disconcerting to our human
pride and folly to our self-esteem, so far counter to our
instincts as to power and our conceits as to wisdom.

Any decision constituting Christianity will seem remote
for many today, not only in the long retrospect of time and
place, but in the utter contrast of a static — not to say
soiled — image. Convention, rather than decision,
characterises an old and tired faith, as many see it. No doubt

tradition, as the initiated know, is a living, vibrant experience,
the pulse of conviction in the bloodstream of community.
But, perceived from without as traditionalism and assump-
tion, it seems to others like the inertia of the closed mind,
the indulgence of an unexamined comfort. Where Christians
of born-again enthusiasm sound decisive enough, they often
seem purveyors of a facile confidence and strangers to all
that agnostics must suspect. Is theirs more a decision in the
emotions than in the mind and will? Are they truly with the
New Testament in all that it entails as a scripture upon its
contemporary people? Is the thought of 'the perennial
decision now' reduced rather to a peripheral decision, an
indulgence for those so minded but hardly relevant to
the mood or movement of the world? Approaching two
thousand years on from what decided Christianity can that
deciding still be sustained?

We have first in reply to face the secular pre-possession
resulting from scientific technology and further application
of technique to the interpretation and manipulation of
society and of the self. Sociology and psychology, aiming to
apply the principles of the physical sciences to the different
worlds of persons in relation, have generated, with their
legitimate uses and analyses, a popular attitude of indifference to other dimensions of experience eluding such
disciplines. Transcendence, poetry, the sense of wonder, the
meaning beyond the explaining — all these are casualties of
the dominance of technique. Not necessarily so, to be sure,
but widely so in the modern idiom. The things of the spirit,
if not ignored, offer dubious, unfamiliar credentials to be
treated, at worst with dismissal, at best with indecision.

In overcoming such attitudes of mind, commendation of
Christian decision has interior problems of its own, which
go beyond the several issues for scholarship earlier
considered. Broadly these are the adverse factor of Christian institutionalism and the hampering confusions which
arise from the language of Christian conviction. Both aspects
of this situation need to be critically addressed.

It may seem odd to account the institutionalising of faith
a handicap. For institutions are indispensable. The forms
of ministry and the means of sacraments have been central

to Christian decision from the outset. Baptism, holy communion and ordination by the 'laying on of hands' have been crucial to the shape of Christian allegiance and personal participation and corporate nurture, in Christ, since the faith originated. With it they had both warrant and role. Indeed there is no point where Christian decision is more surely measured than in the transaction of baptism, no place and time when it is more deeply defined and celebrated than in 'the bread and wine.' It is in these, we may say, that Christian decision is sacramentalised into perpetuity through all the generations.

Ecclesiastical pretensions, however, have long and sadly, illserved these simplicities through the subtle temptations to which all establishments are prone. Rituals can usurp their own meanings in official possessiveness or develop accretions which finally undo them. Clergy too easily become the proprietors rather than the debtors of grace. We lose either the art or the skill to have incidentals be the incidentals they are by a failure to subdue them adequately to the heart of the faith. 'I magnify my office,' writes Paul (Romans 11.13) as well he may. Popes and Patriarchs, Bishops, Priests and Deacons readily do likewise, if with a differing rationale. And well they may. For, without office, how is the truth served or faith commended or fellowship engaged? Yet 'they who serve the greater cause may make the cause serve them,' or if not them, the cause they have identified with themselves. The 'office' they 'magnify' has existence only in the reality of Christ and has, therefore, to be always and only tributary to the central truth. Ministry has perpetual obligation to its own humility — a humility only authentic under the authority of whom it serves. To be apostolic is to be faith-bearing not status mongering. Where it is otherwise its effects are such as to distract and divert the expected credence of the world.

But there are establishments in language as well as in hierarchy, in the fabric of words as well as in the interests of structures. The option of Christian decision is obscured for many by the uncertainty as to its meaning in the terms in which it is housed. The logical positivists are in the wrong in the cruder claims that language meanings are confined to empirically verifiable statement — a delusion which many of them have now outgrown. But there is point in their awareness, and their warning, that usage *per se* can give illusory existence, or distorted identity, to ideas it purveys. Repetition can entrench delusion. We may give pseudo existence to notions merely by repeating names. Or we may fail to register the meaning we are meant to take.

The last is very much a feature of the language of theology and worship. 'Mythology' is a confounding word to use here in respect of Christian doctrine. For its technical sense of storied metaphor is irretrievably lost to its popular mean-ing of fantasy and falsehood. The word still bedevils what needs to be understood and has been maliciously used by those who intended only confusion. Yet what has to be realised behind the malice and confusion is that much in Christian vocabulary, in creed and hymn and prayer, is liable to misconstruing in the day to day world. Further, the necessary effort to correct this is frequently taken for compromise or evasion, while those who undertake the burden of language intelligibility and truthfulness are suspect of disloyalty.

The surest way to grapple with what is here at stake is to keep, as the New Testament does, within a Christology of action, rather than of status, or one of status only on behalf of what the action means. Or, in simpler terms, it is to see the event of Christ-according-to-Jesus as belonging essentially with a living obedience where 'being' is in the 'doing'. The Creeds' word 'substance' in this context ('of one substance with the Father') only has contemporary fitness if we take it in the sense with which, for example, one might say: 'I can substantiate the case I'm making', or the retort: 'There is no substance in your argument.'

These are obvious fields that lie within the obligations of the closing chapter. But associated with them all is the issue which lies precisely in the 'action' by which, in the mind of Jesus' we identify the mind of God. Is that 'harmlessness', that will to suffer, that self-giving at cost into the wrong-doing of a hostile world, credibly viable in the human scene as we know it? How can a crucified Christ ever be other than a contradiction, an illusion, a consolatory wishfulness? Is there not an utter necessity and, therefore, an entire legitimacy in the religious reliance on power? Can faiths expect to escape the compromises required in the politics of force?

It is here that the New Testament faith is in radical distinction from other religious patterns. Certainly Islam assumes without question the propriety of force on behalf of truth. So likewise does Judaism in its Maccabean and Zionist form; Sikhism likewise. Indeed all faiths, including Christianity through much of its history, have adopted belligerence and relied on the sanctions of power and the state. It was quite otherwise, as we have seen, with the event of Jesus as the Christ and with the definitive Gospel of original Christianity. But is that faith in the finality of the love that suffers sustainable still, in the light of its repudiation by the realists of this world? Can 'the God with wounds' be more than a fond paradox, an admirable futility? Must not such Easter faith be seen as either senti-mental or premature? Are we not wiser to leave to mystery and agnosticism the issue between evil and God, rather than to resolve it in the redeeming pain of the Almighty? There can be no doubt about what decided Christianity. But was it ever rightly so? Perhaps all we can say is that if the Christian identification of pain with love and both with God remains a mystery it stands precisely where final mystery needs to be.

A present irrelevance, a sorry confusion, a private indulgence, a forfeited credibility, an idle romanticism, an effete understanding — all these adverse verdicts have been made against the faith which emerged so dramatically in the wake of the Jesus of Galilee and Gethsemane, believed and loved by disciples of his word and deed as the fulfilment of God. They are the verdicts of today's unpersuadedness. To give them due hearing will prove a salutary discipline in the commendation of the faith which hears them out. They will not daunt or deter it in sustaining its first, its present, decision.

CHAPTER 1

The Crucial Happening

The Resurrection — obviously: that is where all began. Easter
was the birthday of the faith. So will many, explaining their
Christianity, expect and be expected to say. But no! We had
better come to Easter by and by, and in its proper context
of before and after. For only in 'before and after' does it
consist at all, being no isolated wonder inexplicably explaining all else. On the contrary it belongs only as a sequel
with a sequel. It may not be isolated from the Gethsemane
of Jesus, just as his Gethsemane may not be severed from
all that transpired out of his Nazareth. Resurrection inaugurated all that followed in the actuality of faith and
fellowship only because these were explicit within the whole
ministry and death of Jesus. Resurrection simply launched
and liberated them into their authentic history.

The geographer needs the Nile to understand its delta,
just as the geologist recognises a volcano by the cone and
crater at its peak. Physical imagery is a feeble parable,
except in suggesting how facts of consequence have consequence within them, consequence on either side of what they
are. So it is with Jesus' Resurrection. We must therefore place
it in the total setting where it belongs and in its great 'before
and after' as these alone disclose its meaning as their climax.

To realise what the crucial happening was we start from
the New Testament as literature and document. What is the
impetus by which it flows? It is clearly a literature of
community and a document about a history. It is not the
product of some private philosophic mind, nor is it the
musings of a mystic spirit. It looks back so firmly to a past
that it does so four times over. But it is concerned for what
is ahead, the stresses mentally and socially present in the
creation of new community. Hence its Epistles, warm with
solicitude for that new society's definition in conduct and

concept. That self-education, in turn, is no abstract con-
jecturing of ideal good or innate wisdom. On the contrary,
it harks back, like needle to its pole, towards the story to which
it knows it owes itself. And it is, in fact, the sole narrator
of that story, the central figure of which it mediates for all
time through the perception of its own conviction. Its
conviction owes itself, in turn, to the history kindling that
perception.

It is important to appreciate that had Jesus been, in fact,
other than this literature lives by, he would never have been
documented or survived into a future. A river — unless it
spends itself in barren sands or struggles only into swamp —
consists within the banks it cuts and fills, just as these, for
their part, contain the flow they receive and so direct. There
is no point in asking about the river except in attention to
its course. In some sense, likewise, we have to ask respecting
Jesus, what was it, how was it, that he came to have this
sequel? To do so will not foreclose all study, as we must
recognise in chapters 3 and 6. But it will remain the primary
criterion inasmuch as it is the only one to yield us data from
which to judge. The very being of the New Testament as
writing by, for and from community in its contents, is the
evidence of the crucial happening we are at pains to
understand.

There is clearly a thrust of dispersion in these contents.
That is plain to see by merely glancing at the addresses of
those missives we call the Epistles — Rome, Corinth, Galatia,
Philippi, Colosse and the rest. But if they go into what the
Greeks called a diaspora, a scattered diversity of provinces
and cities, it is because there is a unity which binds them.
They owe obligation to each other and stand within a
common vocation which necessitates the apostolic nurture
and a central pastoral concern. This mutuality around a
leadership stems from the single story originating them all,
the story in the lively custody of mentors and tutors who
themselves stand within the authority of a history that made
them such.

The Mediterranean world in which these bonds of a single
retrospect were forged was familiar enough with dispersion
and with the possibility of the meeting, in some measure

of concert, of its leading cultures, the Jewish and the Greek.
There was the synagogue movement of Jewish gathering, away
from Jerusalem, around the mystery of Torah. Synagogues
attracted proselytes from among Greeks and Romans and
served the inter-penetration of the Greek and Hebrew worlds.
And there was the Septuagint, one of the finest literary
enterprises of those centuries around the rise of Christianity,
a work which greatly facilitated the expression of Christian
faith and its dissemination.

But all this rich mutual infusion of the Greek and the
Hebraic had its sturdy reservations, its hesitations. Either
party remained tenacious of identity and there was
something essentially irreducible within Jewishness by
virtue of the chosen seed. Hellenistic Judaism did not
admit of an integration which indifferently incorporated Jew
and Gentile. This radical step happened in the context of
faith in Jesus-Messiah. It involved the coining of the new
name of 'Christian' by which fellowship *via* faith was aptly
denoted. A society in which the Jew/Gentile distinction was
transcended had a long and complex struggle with itself to
make the unity intact — a struggle that has left its mark
deeply upon the New Testament's pages. But complex as were
all the attendant questions of Torah and circumcision, of
synagogue and eucharist, they did not leave in doubt the
emphatic unity which posed them. In that 'household of God'
there were 'no more strangers, but only fellow citizens . . .'
(Eph. 2.19), a crucial happening indeed!

It would be naive to think of it as self-explanatory, an odd
surge of passing sentiment. It was a re-writing of 'the
household of God' as hitherto gathered in ethnic quality
around the law of Sinai, where Israel had transacted an
inalienable covenant. It was a strenuous re-siting of rendezvous with God, in fulfilment, to be sure, of the old yet
opening the benediction to all mankind, irrespective of
birth, culture, worth, or dwelling-place. It constituted a
discovery of human community, indifferently to all these
denominators, a discovery prompted by the Christian reading
of the Christian thing which — as 'Christianity' believed —
had happened in, and because, of Jesus.

It is necessary to use the term 'Christian' in this perhaps

novel way. For there could be other 'readings' of what would
then be taken for another 'thing'. These, to be considered
in a later chapter, need not detain us now, since they have
decided against the decision we are studying. Of the 'reading'
and the 'thing' which together give us 'Christianity' the New
Testament is in no doubt. For it actually derives from what
it read. Let us hear from it in one of its most resounding
passages:

> 'The love of Christ makes up our mind when we have
> reached the conclusion that the one man died for all and
> therefore all mankind has died. The reason he died for all
> is that men in their living should no longer be living for
> themselves but to him who for their sake died and was
> raised to life.
> From now on worldly ideas have ceased to count for us in
> esteeming any man. Indeed, they no longer count, as they
> once did, in our estimate of Christ. For anyone who is in
> Christ there is a new creation: the old life is at an end, a new
> one is already begun. All this is the work of God. He has
> reconciled us to Himself through Christ and has given to us
> the ministry of reconciliation. That is to say God was in Christ
> reconciling the world to Himself, not holding men's sins
> against them and has entrusted to us this word of reconcilia-
> tion. So then we are ambassadors on behalf of Christ. It is
> as though God were appealing to you through us: in Christ's
> name we bid you earnestly 'Be reconciled to God.' For he who
> was innocent of sin He made to be one with the sinfulness
> of mankind so that, in him, we might be made one with the
> righteousness of God.'

The writer is Paul but he uses throughout the plural and
claims to be standing in one tradition. We can leave aside
here the suspicion of some that he is 'the villain of the piece,'
the source of an aberration that has led to a misconstruing
of Jesus. There is no such confusion in the ardent thrust and
logic of this passage. In its insistent 'we have concluded . . .'
'we are ambassadors . . .' 'we appeal . . .' 'ceased to count for
us . . .' it echoes the community with which we began. But
that unity of conviction and appeal springs directly from
'the work of God.' That 'work' which has changed their whole
perspective is achieved in Jesus as the realisation of
Messiahship, makng Jesus the Christ, and it is said to be
decisively the act of God.

The reaching of this conclusion brought a radically new comprehension of what such Messiahship entailed and how it had been realised. Old perceptions are seen as worldly-wise, and resting on categories — such as race, force, flamboyant power, separatist sanctity, apocalyptic inter-vention — now made obsolete by the new, the actual, Christhood which discarded them all and moved instead through suffering to reconciliation.

That revolution in hope was brought about in the action of Jesus, and is accredited to God Himself, acting 'in Christ in order to reconcile.' The claim is that when we can identify the Christ we have the context where the vital clue for our understanding of God is to be found. In that action of Jesus we know God for who He is. Our right so to believe is grounded in the fact that the thought of Messiah arises only in the context of faith in those other credentials of God believed to be present in the fact of creation and of cove-nant. For it is these which give the right to hope that a divine responsibility is involved in human history. Awaiting Messiah is trusting that responsibility: identifying Messiah is acknowledging where it is fulfilled.

The study of all the varieties of Messianic prospect which this requires is deferred to chapter 2. It is the Christian conclusion which concerns us now with 2 Cor. 5.14-21 as guide. Nowhere in the New Testament is its logic more dramatically stated within the consensus of the whole Scripture. 'The love of Christ' has resolved perplexity and clinched decision. The Greek verb in v.14 has the sense of a thronging crowd holding someone under pressure, as when the people were congested around Jesus in the incident of the woman who 'touched the hem of his garment.' It was all she could do in the press around him. Or the verb is needed when 'Jerusalem is compassed with armies.' Such constraint decides all options: it leaves us no longer to our own devices but lays us under a necessity we must concede. But since it is love which does so, it is no tyranny: it is just the irresistibility — to change the metaphor — of the case we must allow. There is a consensus about a conclusion and neither leaves us free to disallow the other. So Paul.

The consensus and conclusion convey us into ministry with

a message, a message intending the human whole. This
ministry is to be discharged as living proxy for Christ himself.
The appeal is his alone but it is we who are to bring it,
being in ourselves the evidence for what we tell. It is plain
to see how in all these aspects the Resurrection is explicit,
not as a strange phenomenon on its own, but in the sense
of a Christ moving into universality through a living
community charged with the meaning of his death. These —
impulse, commission, fellowship and the trust of truth —
are all the marks of a risen Jesus, alive in these terms for
evermore. In this way the passage captures the experience
which made the New Testament.

But what is this 'reconciliation' of which it tells and how
is it related to the suffering which kindles the love and sets
the constraints? How could it be said to consist in, and
proceed from, a crucified Messiah? The Greek noun *katallage*
means to bring a party from a state of enmity into a state
of amity by an act of pardon and forgiveness — an act in
which acceptance is offered and acceptance is received. The
initiative is always costly because, foregoing hatred and
rejection, it undertakes to bear the wrong which alienation
would perpetuate. The taking is always humbling because
it requires what we are conditioned to resist, namely
penitence, humility, self-reproach and contrition. In paying
its own cost 'reconciliation' seals our readiness to cease such
resistance within ourselves, salutes us in the new quality of
honesty and confirms it by restoring what estrangement had
broken. It is from the wound that healing is found.

Christianity came about in the realisation that exactly this
had happened between God and humanity. The wound and
the healing were present in the Cross of Jesus. How was God
in the reconciling there? — because Messiah and Messiahship
were God's prescript about our humanity at odds with Him.
How were the reconciled there? — because the way they were
at odds with Him had declared itself in crucifying Jesus. How,
then, was the reconciliation present? — because of how
Messiah-Jesus had offered and expressed it in the manner
of his suffering. Here, in the history that made them, lay the
secret by which it did so. The event issued into the experience
and the experience interpreted and possessed it. On both

counts it was decisive, decisive for how they were to think
of God and how they were to relate to the world.

What then of the language in which they were to do so?
For language is vital both to inward conviction and its
communication. The first Christians had much imagery to
hand in their familiar setting. There was, instinctively, the
metaphor of sacrifice. The Cross of Jesus had happened
within a stone's throw of the walls of the holy city and its
sacred Temple. The garden of his agony across the Kedron
valley lay, at sunset, almost in the Temple's shadow. The terms
of cleansing in the ancient ritual suggested how reconciliation might be understood. In due course the Epistle to the
Hebrews would sound a warning about how hopelessly
inadequate such analogy must be — a warning which some
later theologies have been slow to heed. For language about
'the lamb who was slain' and 'the blood which cleanses from
all sin' would be sadly distorting — as indeed all metaphor is
— unless properly disciplined and read within its limits.

For no 'lamb' ever faced a Gethsemane in conscious
surrender to vocation. Only words like 'the cup my Father
has given me' suffice that situation. 'Led like a lamb to the
slaughter' would be true of Jesus in terms of victimisation.
But the actual narrative of the arrest denies it by the quality
of command and dignity in which he faced the 'band with
swords and staves' and checked the impulsive Peter. Nevertheless the rites of the altar might dimly and darkly intimate
the larger meaning of his self-surrender. And since
vocabulary is for communication it has to be in the hearers'
world as well as on the speaking lips.

The 'lamb' language had truer resonance when it derived
from the precedent of the suffering prophets, Jeremiah most
of all. They had endured 'the contradiction of sinners against
themselves', the tragic role of truthbearers in a hostile society.
The mysterious 'suffering servant' in Isaiah 42-53 was the
most telling focus of this theme, fulfilling while transcending the metaphors of oblation borrowed to describe him
from the sheepfolds that fed the Temple altars. Such
precedent, it seems clear, weighed heavily with Jesus in his
Jerusalem. It was, therefore, instinctive for the disciples to tell
of him in the same idiom of sacrifice and innocence for sin.

This setting of prophetic suffering, furthermore, led into the vocabulary of vindication. 'The just man' wrote Habakkuk, 'was justified by his fidelity.' (Hab. 2.4). Abrahamic tradition hinted the same. Vindication of faithful souls, like Jeremiah, who endured obloquy and scorn in their loyalty to truth, lay simply in the fact that by their tenacity they vindicated God. It lay not merely in whether their warnings came true, but rather in that they ensured the truth out-lasting all apostasy. So doing, their costly loyalty, in the event, proved the salvation even of those who reviled and oppressed them. What men cruelly did to them became the means whereby what they achieved for men emerged out of tragedy into an inclusive benediction. Even the maligners and tormentors would confess: 'with their stripes we are healed.' For, in the sufferers, integrity was crucially and triumphantly tested. In their life-story truth itself had undergone its own crisis and prevailed.

How fitting that this theme of vindication should come into its own when the disciples, kindled by the Resurrection, began to discern the crisis in the life-story of Jesus as both fitting and enlarging those precedents. Paul cites the prophet Habakkuk's summary of the travail for truth inseparable from its faithful confession. But he does so only to move beyond what Habakkuk had said. That 'the just — or righteous — man shall live by his faithfulness' (Hab. 2.4) was one thing. That 'by his faith (i.e. by belief in Jesus) a man is made just (i.e. justified)' (Romans 3.28 and elsewhere) was another. Paul quotes, as it were, only to misquote. Yet the movement in his mind is a vital clue to Christianity. What precisely was the progression in his argument?

The point of departure is prophetic fortitude through adversity sustained on behalf of the cause of truth. By such costly fortitude alone is the truth upheld in the context of denial and hatred of it. Such denial and hatred are, in paradox, the tribute of wrong to how true the truth is. For truth is not a passive, abstract thing: it is a verdict on behalf of God against all that disavows it. The suffering truth entails on those who serve it — given the way the world is in its wrongfulness — is the form in which truth prevails. Prevailing in those terms — and only those — it is able to hold itself inviolate. So doing, and by so doing not being overcome of evil, it is able to outlast and outdo the wrong and incorporate the wrongdoers, on the condition of repentance, into its own untarnished, undefeated benediction.

That vital condition of repentance its very suffering has the power to kindle and constrain. For truth, as by example, in 'the suffering servant' of Isaiah 42 and 53, has not only suffered because of, and against, all its adversaries. It has suffered on behalf of them. It is only suffering love, in the behalf of truth, which has this capacity to be both against, and for, the evildoers of the world. To have realised that this was how it was in and at the Cross of Jesus was to have discovered Christianity. By identifying a principle Paul realised a Gospel.

The travail of the prophets, he saw, had been solitary yet vicarious. Intimate and tragic to them, the cost of sustaining truth's cause became redemptive for all when each and all perceived it so. Without that perception the fact and the meaning would remain unrecognised. But they would still be there, unwearied, uncoercive, and, therefore, undefeated. For 'responding love transfigures what it bears,' and there is, finally, no other way of 'overcoming evil with good,' or of overcoming evil at all. Or, phrasing this in personal language as the Isaiah passages do about 'the suffering servant,' we come to acknowledge how 'he was wounded for our transgressions' and that 'with his stripes we are healed.' (Isaiah 53.5). It is because of him that we confess: 'All we like sheep had gone astray.' (Isa. 53.6). To perceive it so is to stand in its meaning. Redeeming suffering condemns what we have been but only in releasing us from it.

This is the secret which lies at the heart of what Christianity understands by 'God in Christ reconciling the world.' It is what warrants and undergirds faith in the Incarnation. To see how evil situations inflict suffering, to discover how such suffering taken up into love masters the situations, and to believe that it was even so with God as disclosed in a drama of His authorship at the Cross — this was, and is, to find oneself Christian. Believing thus about Jesus and his death became a faith to save those believing. The *fidelity* of Jesus passed into the *faith* concerning him, with suffering for truth the clue to the sequence. The justifying intrinsic to faithful prophets became by grace the justification of those who by faith knew it so in Jesus. So Paul, so the first Christians. Jesus, they said, was 'made intimate with sin' through the enmity of men that we 'might be made righteous before God through him.' Though analogies from law courts have come into this understanding, it is clear that this reconciliation is no arbitrary acquittal, no kind of legal fiction, releasing x on the ground of incriminating y. To read this way would be a travesty of what faith had understood about vicarious suffering and those 'men of sorrows.' There was nothing suppositious about the way in which the crucified was caught up into the world's sinfulness, nor yet about the way in which his acceptance of that fact took up the sinful into its forgiveness.

There was, and is, no arbitrary transference of guilt, though ill-used animal metaphors have sometimes suggested this. The guilt of the wrongful was emphatically their own, whether in violating the prophets or crucifying the Christ. What was transferred happened in these sufferers for truth becoming vulnerable, for love's sake. Healing was where the wounds were. Popular mentality might sometimes cause the meaning of this realisation to turn later into some merely formal credence, glibly told, at times, in some citations of: 'Believe on the Lord Jesus Christ and you will be saved.' (Acts 16.31). But with Paul and his hearers, and the dazed and desperate gaoler at Philippi, it was anything but formal. It meant an act of trusting, of accepting to be accepted, of justifying the love by which one is justified.

From faith's acceptance to be so forgiven, in these terms and cost, came the will to righteousness, as the proof, not the purchase, of justification. Self-reproach had surely, in Jesus' parable, a different quality on the morrow of 'the best robe, the ring on the hand and the shoes on the feet.' Justification was the lifting of a charge only in being a leavening of the life. Such personal revolution could readily be expressed in early Christian vocabulary by the imagery of washing, and so of baptism. The elementary sense of cleansing a fabric — still itself yet newly so — had even fuller import when water in washing was associated with the waters of the Red Sea and the Jordan as the Hebraic Rubicon, or decisive crossing from the old and into the new.

Such 'washing of regeneration,' as Titus 3.5 phrased it, could well marry with Paul's analogy of 'the old Adam,' the 'natural' man, made anew 'in Christ.' 'Old things' thus 'passed away and all things became new' in personal life as well as in Messianic expectation.

Or there was another more charming idiom by which to tell the event-experience we are exploring. The Hebrew tradition was deeply imbued with the thought of 'the divine countenance.' The blessing given to Aaron in Numbers (6.24-26) by Moses from God to pronounce over the people had the fourfold: 'The Lord bless and keep . . . make His face to shine upon you . . . lift upon you the light of His face . . . and give you peace.' The yearning of the psalmists echoes the words (e.g. 4.6, 89.15, and 90.8). Paul in 2 Cor. 4.6 is bold to find them fulfilled in 'the face of Jesus Christ,' where, he says: 'We have the light of the knowledge of the glory of God.' In the significance of Jesus he reads the realisation of the Aaronic blessing. By the 'face' he means the whole reality. Faces are where identities are known. In paraphrase we may say: 'what a face is to a personality Jesus is to God.' And how deep a parable that is of what the faith understood by incarnation. There is nothing more fragile, sensitive, revelatory, mobile, than facial features — a fabric of nerve, sinew, muscle, skin, so sweetly joyous, so sadly marred, across which move and pass, or haunt and stay, a medley of emotions — fear, hope, surprise, anguish, despair, anger, perplexity, scorn, pity, cunning, joy, doubt, wistfulness, turmoil and serenity. And a life's history may be written there, and read. There is no more apt incarnation, the physical and the spiritual in one intimacy. Aaron, like the poet Browning with his: 'Face My hands fashioned see it in Myself,' was well taught to invoke 'the countenance divine.' And Paul in the New Testament was well inspired to think the invocation realised in the implications of Jesus in the reality of event-experience, the face knowable and the face known.

Writing to the Christians at Corinth (1 Cor. 3.23), Paul tells

them: 'All things are yours, you are Christ's and Christ is
God's.' What, we might ask, is the missing final word? or is
there one? Does he leave the noun possessed to be supplied?
If so, 'God's Son' would be the doctrinal answer enjoined
by orthodoxy. But, if this becomes a bare formula doing
duty for comprehension, it will simply push the question
further. To say 'God's Messiah' after 'Christ is . . .' would be
simply a predicate repeating the subject. Would 'God's
answer' be appropriate? To be sure it would, precisely if we
know to what question. (a theme for chapter 2). 'God's policy,'
might suffice; 'God's poetry' would be true; 'God's signature'
likewise; and in all these ways with John's approval: 'God's
Word.' The crucial meaning, surely, is a Christ 'according to
God' and, therefore, 'God according to Christ.' The first
Christians could not rightly have believed as they did
concerning Jesus and his Cross, if they had not believed him
so because of God.

The Fourth Gospel, it would be true to say, supplies Paul's
missing word in 1 Cor. 3.23, with its own characteristic term
doxa, or 'glory,' the very word Paul, too, employed in the
passage about 'the face of Christ.' In both alike *doxa* (as its
borrowing by the English word 'orthodoxy' tells) means right
and true conceptions and these, for theology, must always
mean 'doxology,' the celebration of the infinitely worthy.
Nowhere are we nearer to the decisiveness of Christianity
than here. It was in their perception of the meaning of the
Cross that the first Christians read the clue to the divine glory.
Throughout, in all their writings, in Luke and John and Peter
pre-eminently, the suffering and the glory define each other
and belong in one. 'Father, glorify Thy Name' is how the
fourth evangelist reads, in Jesus' prayer, the secret of
Gethsemane. 'We beheld his glory' is his summation in the
Prologue. So he can understand Jesus in the words that are
at once prospect to the Cross and retrospect over
Messiahship: 'The glory Thou gavest me I have given to them.'
It was the gift, we may say, of being Christian. It conferred
an identity but only through and from the identity of Christ
as he in whom and from whom was known the identity of
God. It was a disclosure which evoked a decision, a decision
standing in discovery.

'The suffering and the glory' is the formula both in the
Gospel and the Acts from the pen of Luke, who associates
these together, with those precedents from prophetic history
we have noted. How tenderly this emerges in the familiar
passage at the end of Luke's Gospel concerning the two
disciples en route to Emmaus — one of the most revealing
passages about the nature of the Resurrection. 'Ought *not*
the Christ to have suffered these things and to enter into
his glory'? it has the risen Master ask. The question indicates
that it expects the answer Yes! But on every mundane count
of this-worldly wisdom the answer must be No! Indeed the
question should be turned around and become an exclama-
tion: 'Ought the Christ to have suffered these things?!' The
Christ? How could he save others who could not even save
himself? His followers, as Peter seems to be suggesting in the
celebrated exchange in Matthew 16.21-23 with his 'This shall
never be *to you,*' might be expendable pawns, but never the
Messiah himself. The Gospel narratives muse on the taunts
at the crucifixion for the same reason: 'Let him save
himself . . .' And — immediate considerations apart — the
very fact of being crucified was, conceptually, itself a disproof
of Messianic status, an effrontery and offence against all the
susceptibilities of Jewish feeling.

Yet, against the grain of tenacious instinct and all
practical criteria of what it takes to save, it was the wounds
that won the day both in the economy of God and the
conviction of the disciples. This *was* resurrection. The Christ
ought to have suffered in that, suffering apart, evil is never
retrieved. All the alternatives to the pattern of the Cross —
whether stoic indifference and sheer endurance, or perpetual
enmity, retaliation, requital, or despairing capitulation,
only leave the evil either where it was or accentuated and
intensified. Only bearing bears away. It is precisely this
paradox which is caught in the very word in the Greek, *airon,*
of John 1.29. The disciples, as Jews, could not have come upon
this perception, with all its disconcerting authenticity, by
some strange aberration of mind, some odd logic of their
own. Nor could it have come to them in some context of
unrelieved despair and desolation. It belonged only with the
living reality of Jesus as the Christ by virtue of the Cross,

first known to them as desolation, now disclosed to them as glory.

Peter, who according to the evangelists had known that desolation most desperately, fills his First Epistle with his own witness to the same theme. He makes it the pattern by which to sustain and hearten the tribulation of those to whom he writes. 'Inasmuch as Christ has suffered,' he says, 'arm yourselves with the same mind.' They are enabled to bear and to renounce evil in being themselves healed by the wounds of Jesus. He recalls with the vividness of the mind's eye the demeanour of Jesus in the presence of Pilate (2.22-25). Jesus suffered, he tells them, 'the just for the unjust to bring us to God.' 'To bring us to God' is the very heart of the matter — to God as we must conceive of Him, to God as we may think and know Him, to God in the terms that are given to us in Jesus. This experience Peter makes the ground of all he has to say to his readers about their own fortitude in circumstances where 'suffering as a Christian' is the likeliest thing to happen to them. (4.16).

In this consensus of the language of the New Testament we find the experience which first defined Christianity, inasmuch as those who knew it so and told it so became Christians in so doing. They became who they were in the coming to be of the literature of their genesis. Both they, and it, inseparably, derive from Jesus as the Christ perceived as such by them in faith and love. We have to say that it was a decision which realised itself as it went along. It was dramatic in respect of its radical quality but it was also cumulative as a steady education into its fulness. We can see that it was no sanguine faith, able to believe only because it had first superficialised what was — and is — at stake in believing at all. On the contrary, its point of departure and its controlling theme had to do with a situation which plumbed the depths of perplexity and despair. The same world which had heard the Sermon on the Mount had reared the Cross. It was a world about which there could be no illusions, but a world which could recognise in both Sermon and Cross the answer to the worst about it.

It would be possible to comprehend the gist of this Christianity, *via* Christians because of Christ, in the single

cherished Hebraic word so familiar to them all, the word
AMEN. For it has the double meaning of: 'It is so, let it be
so.' It is at once affirming and letting be what is affirmed.
What is has to be allowed to be. Such is the case with actuality
in many ordinary spheres of life. When some role or office
is designated — be it ambassador, or constable, or priest, or
magistrate — recognition of the fact means responding to
the function. The love in marriage which makes a couple
husband and wife in mutual status-giving requires and frees
them to fulfill what they are. What, as lawyers say, is *de jure*
is then *de facto*, while *de facto* implements *de jure*. There is a
kind of Amen here: 'We are, let us be . . .' The actuality is
at once fact and fulfilment of fact and neither, in a bonded
context, without the other.

It was likewise with the commitment we are studying which
decided Christianity. The words 'Amen, Amen I say to you'
had prefaced much of the teaching of Jesus. 'The Amen'
became one of his titles in the Book of Revelation. The Christ,
who truly was so, had to be allowed to be so in the allegiance
of the will and the greeting of the spirit. And this is how
it was in the fervour of the Epistles, those documents which
saw nurture within the churches as a translation of fact-actual
into fact-effective. Christians, each and all, had to become
what, or rather who, they already were, the act of faith
being fulfilled in the work of faith. The process was continual
only because it was begun. Both faith and ministry, Paul
insisted in 2. Cor. 1 were 'not Yes and No, but Yes.'

We can capture this quality of things in another turn of
phrase in the New Testament: '. . . but now . . .' where the
writers mark the contrast between what used to be and what
has come to be, between former notions of community and
those which now prevail. They had been 'strangers and
foreigners' in Ephesus, 'but now' they are so no longer. (Eph.
2.13-18). For the new faith had not secured itself in any privacy
of exemption from mankind. Its people had a dubious manner of life 'but now' says Colossians 3.8, they had 'shed those
ways.' It is a refrain which echoes through all the Epistles.
Galatians 4.9 makes it an urgent plea when elements of the
transformation are put in danger by compromise. 1 Peter
rejoices in those who once 'were not a people but now' have

become so, who once were astray 'but now' have come home
(2.10 and 25). 'But now we see Jesus crowned,' writes the
author of Hebrews, 'but now Christ has put away sin by the
sacrifice of himself' (2.8 and 9.26). Grace was once hidden
'but is now made manifest,' says 2. Tim. 1.10. Passages in
Romans reverberate with the same decisive sense of event
and experience (3.21, 6.22, 7.6 and 16.26), likewise
1 Corinthians (7.14, 12.18 and 12.20), while 1 John has a lively
stress on what is now in contrast to a hitherto which lacked it.

But the most resounding of them all is that in 1 Corinthians 15.20 where a great argument of Paul reaches its climax:
'But now is Christ risen from the dead.' It was right that we
should reach the Resurrection by the road we have taken,
a road conveying us through this actual territory of event
and experience, as reciprocal the one to the other. For Easter
does not celebrate an unrelated marvel incongruously
warranting an extraneous trust. On the contrary, it consists
in the divine *imprimatur* on the significance of Jesus crucified
and in the realisation of that significance of which the
Resurrection was both the occasion and the symbol.

The Gospels lay careful emphasis on the fact and the
manner of Jesus' burial. The Creeds, later, are equally
emphatic in the words: 'crucified, dead and buried,' and
'suffered and was buried.' The faith has always had place for
the tomb. And 'the grave', as the poet had it, is indeed 'a fine
and private place', a narrow place that says 'Finis' and is
'deprived' of life. So it was with Jesus in the wake of crucifixion. There was nothing illusory about his death or Joseph
of Arimathea's sepulchre on loan. In that dimension of the
Gospels and the Creeds we are in the physical world of place
and fact. But when we move to Jesus exaltation, to the
language, for example, of Phil. 2 9: 'God has highly exalted
him . . .' we are in a different realm. The meaning of Christ's
Ascension does not entail a space journey. We have passed
into the realm of metaphor, of sovereignty, authority and
transcendence, of the right to reign. These are no less
factual for their not being physical.

The event of the Resurrection stands between the two
realms, between a grave in a garden and a throne in heaven.
It belongs with both and partakes of each. This is its dual

quality. There are many times — as in Phil. 2 and Hebrews throughout — where resurrection and ascension are seen as one, the former completely taken into the significance of the latter. Yet inescapably that significance is tethered to a burial and a grave. The Gospel narratives, heavily stylised as they are, and using evocative imagery, are nevertheless firmly centred in the real garden and telling of a tomb with grave-clothes and intending embalmers. The truth of Easter has to belong with both worlds, intervening between an actual burial and a spiritual enthronement, between physical demise and eternal authority.

It is here that the tomb's emptiness has its necessary part in the narrative. Its significance is best captured in the decisive negative: 'He is *not* here.' Were the 'not' elided, so that 'he was there' the Easter meaning would be discredited on its Cross-ward side and, therefore, on its other side as well. Given that there were powerful forces eager to extinguish the Gospel of the Resurrection, and given that the surest way to do so would have been to produce and placard a corpse, it is reasonable to assume that, had they been able, they would certainly have done so. To have done so, equally certainly, would have been to terminate the incipient faith and to obviate any necessity of deterring it — hopelessly as it proved — by persecution. By that logic it would be right, further, to conclude that 'he was not there.' But non-location of a corpse is not the Easter fact. The tomb *could* have been 'empty' being mis-identified, or — as Matthew has the soldiers being bribed to say — by filching of the body. The urgency of disproving the 'Christians', however, would argue that these perhapses would have been thoroughly investigated and resolved.

The faith in Jesus' Resurrection can appreciate the fact that any such investigation failed to establish any of those perhapses to its own disproof, but it does not rest upon it. That faith apart, such non-solution to a physical mystery would merely constitute a continuing riddle. Furthermore, the positive implication of such non-solution of the physical mystery, namely that the emptiness resulted from resurrection, would still be only on the burial side of the situation. The Resurrection itself can only be rightly understood on

the spiritual side, as the entry into sovereignty and lordship.
All an empty tomb would signify, in isolation, would be an
enigma for detectives. Christian faith did not originate from
an unlocated corpse or the mislaid tenant of a sepulchre.
The evidence of 'he is not here' is only prelude to the
assurance 'he is risen,' the assurance whose literature we have
been learning throughout this chapter.

Nevertheless, the negative 'he is not here' — given the
positive experience — has its place and bearing on the faith.
As a situation, a circumstance within a whole, it dramatically coincides with and sustains the entire assurance from
which the Church began. It does so, provided always that we
recognise how it could, as a circumstance, be explained
otherwise than that assurance holds. The honesty of such
recognition allows it to take its place in faith's confidence
without thereby being faith's true or sufficient ground —
ground which only the living Jesus could afford.

Perhaps the point here could be indicated by an analogy
from art. The beauty of a Rembrandt portrait or the frown
of a Van Gogh landscape exist in the fabric of canvas and
the substance of oils and pigments. Museumists might be
interested in subjecting these to microscopic scrutiny, but
they would not understand the art that way. To know it they
must stand away and comprehend the whole. Detective work
is not perception of joy or tragedy, whether in respect of
pictures or sepulchres. Yet, were the fabric torn and broken
or the pigments chemically changed, the artistry would be
violated and denied its message. Comparably, as long as the
emptiness of the tomb in the garden is not negated by such
devices, it abides as the otherwise vulnerable fabric of the
artistry of resurrection. Like the material of the artist, it may
serve as the locale or residence of the meaning that inhabits
it as more and different — the reality of the risen Christ.
It is the inter-face between 'crucified, dead and buried' and
'alive for evermore.'

It would be right to say that in the New Testament literature
the apostles were writing their autobiography, but doing so
interleaved with the story of their Master. The words 'death'
and 'dominion' are to the fore in both stories. 'Dominion'
belongs to death in the fact of mortality and sin. But that

'dominion' is broken by a death in which the sin of this mortal world is met and overcome by the love that bears and bears away. 'Dominion' passes to the keeping of that love and is known to do so by disciples who experience again the presence they had known, and known in unawareness of the meaning of the crisis to which it led them, until the issue of the crisis brought its own disclosure.

The Resurrection was not witnessed as a happening. It was perceived as truth. 'The stone was rolled away,' a telling detail in the Gospels, not for escape but for symbol, not by hands intent on conspiracy or compassion — for these alike assumed the stone would baulk them — but by authority of the new 'dominion.' Yet the evidence of that symbol, initially and in its physical starkness, was only distressing and oppressive until its meaning was interpreted in encounter with the Lord.

By warrant of Luke's writing, the calendar of Christian liturgy fits that encounter into a sequence of forty days. He wrote with a retrospect of perhaps forty years. It is well to have the years in view if we are to comprehend what he encloses in the days, namely a conviction of the Lordship of the crucified Jesus, and education into its charge upon disciples, and a realisation that their mission was now the form and context of his ongoing presence. The 'tarrying' from Easter until Pentecost must be understood as enshrining those longer dimensions of discovery. For the narrative lives by the experience of hindsight, of actual departure into the wider world, of liberated minds and tongues, of gathering corroboration of the authentic Christhood and their sure commission. The story of an ending, described in the appearances and the mandating, belongs only with the story of beginnings carrying the apostles from Jerusalem to Antioch and parts beyond — beginnings which had made them surprising to themselves in the breadth and depth of their witness and their ambition. It is that focus of the decades which carries back into the telling of the origins. For the sense of an ending, of an issue, is a privilege of narrative had only by the actors in the going and the doing. Once history has been lived in deed it can be told in prose and symbol.

It is this perspective which enables us to appreciate the empty sepulchre and to comprehend a risen Lord. It is the key to the language with which the Gospels records them. For Gospel description had in view the menace of a persistent cast of mind obtaining in some quarters as the decades lengthened. It was pattern of thought which stemmed from familiar Greek ideas of the transcendent and of the material world, and was prone to disavow the real-ness of the flesh and history. It preferred to visualise the Redeemer as some celestial visitant descending out of the pure realm of spirit and only apparently belonging in the actual world of place and time. The Jesus of such imagining was a masquerade, his suffering only a fantasy to satisfy credulous minds in the realm of 'seeming' alone. By eluding the actual in this guise of the apparent, the divine remained splendidly immune from the soiling, moiling, toiling experience of the human scene. For those of this gnostic bent, Jesus could even be depicted as having his frustrated captors in secret derision while he assured his disciples, from a safe distance, that Calvary was pure charade.

In the light of such fantasies about fantasy it was no less important for the first Christians that the tomb was truly tenanted than that it was seen to be vacated. 'They beheld where he was laid.' They prepared real winding sheets: they intended to embalm. It was in emphasis on this acutality of Christ's suffering and death, and the reality of human fact as the point of divine action, that the Gospels write of food partaken and wound-prints examined. Thomas and the Emmaus road take their place in the immediate story from the concern of the long perspective.

For, if the 'unrealistics', the 'docetics (as Church history knows them) had succeeded in etherealising the Christ the whole theology of the Incarnation and of grace would have been forfeit. As the Epistle to the Hebrews wrote, after some forty years: 'It became Him, from whom are all things, and by whom are all things, in bringing many sons to glory, to make the captain (the architect) of their salvation perfect through suffering.' (Hebrews 2.10). Such 'realism' was appropriate to God. Eternal glory and an actual Gethsemane coincide in His economy. The actuality of the Cross and the

grave was index to the sovereignty of God. Any fantasy of
the one would spell denial of the other. So the faith
believed. That same Letter to the Hebrews in the idiom of
the time had employed the role of angels, in chapter 1, in
expounding the stature of 'the Son.' For the writer shared —
as John Milton did — the imagery of divine majesty attended and obeyed by emissaries and ministrants in 'thousands
at His bidding.' Were not these summoned by prophet and
in psalm — and, indeed in the Qur'ān — to acknowledge in
worship the creature man as trustee of divine 'dominion' in
the natural world and in history? Was it surprising, then,
that the evangelists should tell of angels in attendance on
the victory of resurrrection?

It is ironical that the narrative features in the Gospels
which perplex and dismay the literalists are precisely those
intended to confute the purveyors of unreality in the drama
of redemption. The significance of grave-clothes left behind
in the manner the Fourth Gospel portrays has to be
understood from the fact, not the fantasy, of a corpse from
a cross that needed them. It might seem, momentarily, that
in this particular, the evangelist himself has succumbed to
a philosophy of gnostic mystery for which 'bodies' were no
longer bodies at all. But, in that event, grave-clothes would
never have been a datum, nor a feature of the story. The
question at Easter: 'Why seek the living among the dead?'
would rather have been: 'Why seek the real in the illusory?'

The situation here is sweetly reflected in John's narrative
of Mary Magdalene in the garden (Chap. 20.11-18). and her
encounter with 'the gardener.' However distraught her mind,
the supposition she made was real enough. Gardens do have
gardeners, and maybe Joseph of Arimathea's servant — if
such he was — had assumed a temporary burial and had
expedited the departure of the transient tenant of his
master's costly 'new tomb.' 'If you have borne him hence' has
a strangely haunting ring. For, according to Luke in Acts
(2.24), 'it was not possible' for Jesus to be for long prisoner
of the place. In any event, the mistake in identity is real
circumstance. Yet there follows Mary's recognition of Jesus
that seemingly forbidding: *Noli me tangere,* as the Latin has
it, 'Do not clasp me. For I have not yet ascended to my Father.'

There is no repelling of Mary here. Nor can the sense be
that her embrace somehow prevents what must ensue. He
does not say: 'Do not cling to me because I am ascending . . !
There will still be a personal devotion, an intimate communion, in that future. Ascension does not mean bereavement.
But devotion will not be the same local, immediate bond
in the seen and tangible (cf. the verb in the verse). It will
be in the abiding perpetuation of the presence in an
omnipresence, a sharing with the world of the newly known
implications of all that had once been, in the company of
a Master and the days of his ministry.

Both sides of the grave are in that encounter. The one that
abides into the future is in the idiom of that one that was
realised in the prelude from the past. The Resurrection is
the end in the beginning. It is everywhere in the Gospels
interpreted as the prospect which retrospect has learned.
And we know from what distance of discovery and reflection John the evangelist was writing. The story of Mary holds
the meaning of that contemplation captured in the setting
of the garden and the drama of another soul.

We must return in later chapters to other aspects of this
situation. Our present concern has been with the event-
experience from which the New Testament as a literature of
faith derives. Let us leave the crucial happening here, on the
threshold of its future in the telling of the faith. We must
now turn back to explore the Messianic dimension which
has been central throughout. We must review its sources in
Hebraic tradition, its place in the ministry of Jesus and its
sequel in the shape of Christianity. We can anticipate a task
whose duties are as fascinating as they are exacting.

CHAPTER 2

The Christ-shaped Story

In the sequence of past into present and of present into future what is the principle of hope? And when hope is deferred or denied, what is the ground of patience? There are modern minds who hold that technology and expertise have made all present and future problems soluble — in respect of necessary techniques. But these, alas, do not reckon with the human perversities which all too readily turn feasible panaceas into menaces, blighting or burdening themselves afresh with their own solutions, and hope has to go on living with frustration. In the Graeco-Roman world there were celebrated philosophers who could contrive the ideal society but only by an élitism which must exclude the masses and confine the blessedness to a mind-set and a life-style sustained by those who could not ever share it. Or in the same world there were those who indulged fantasies and dreams of hope, idyllic only by being private, blissful indeed but also fabulous. 'The Graeco-Roman world,' as a historian remarked, 'never achieved a successful image of the Kingdom of Heaven.'

Jews believed they did, or at least one that would be successful, given time. Their principle of hope was Messianic expectation. 'The anointed one' was their ground of patience. For some in contemporary Judaism the principle of hope has been paradoxically translated into a perpetual 'never-Messiah' for hope's own sake. 'Messiah identified,' wrote Martin Buber in Jerusalem, 'is Messiahship betrayed.' For what we can identify and say: 'This is he: this is it' we then no longer await, and since every alleged fulfilment must then foreclose the possibilities we must opt only for a futurism which keeps hope alive by ever denying it a present actuality. This may be heroism and it can claim its own kind of patience, but it could seem to others a nice device for self-delusion which might bring it near to the mind of secular writers like Albert Camus for whom futility and absurdity are only belied because we opt to exclude them.

But such permanent futurism was certainly not the age-long shape of the Messianic dimension in Jewry. It is their eager yearning for the Messianic day, the Messianic climax, the Messianic agency, which we now have to study as entering into the fabric, not to say the very name, of Christianity. We need to trace that dimension to its roots in the whole Hebraic sense of God and history, then to explore it as the setting of Jesus' ministry. Thirdly we have to measure how it was defined and achieved — as Christians believe — in the suffering which crowned that ministry, and the future that crown of suffering gave to it in the Christian community. For it is in all three senses that 'a Christ-shaped story' was the making of Christianity, as 'the image of the Kingdom of heaven' according to Jesus from Galilee to Gethsemane.

Throughout it is important, if obvious, to appreciate that 'the Christ' is in a word of Greek origin what *Mashiah* is in Hebrew. In the course of time the words 'Jesus the Christ' came to have a wholly Christian connotation and 'the' was frequently elided and Messianic identity simply absorbed into a personal name. It is necessary to disallow that usage and keep the name Jesus and the title of 'the Christ' duly distinct.

What, then, was this Christhood central to the fact of Jesus and the theme of all he became in Christianity? There are, it is true, those who question whether the Messianic motif should be taken as index at all. There are others who puzzle themselves about how it was related to Jesus' self-consciousness in the circumstances of his preaching and ministry. These matters we defer to chapter 6. Devaluing of the entire Messianic 'idea', whether Jewish or other, can be better addressed when we have reckoned with it confidently as the legitimate clue both to his story and to its sequel in the Church.

To have it in perspective we have to reach back to 'In the beginning God created . . .' in Genesis 1. 'Beginning' here is not 'the start,' but 'the initiative.' Faith in creation has to do with a divine intention in the world, a purposiveness of which man is the crux. It is, of course, possible to see this conviction as simply the projection on to the whole of our evident experience of the part, or — as Feuerbach had it — divine purpose is merely human subjectivity writ large. From our infancy we assume meaning and take what we experience as a domain we explore, interrogate, assume to signify, find — in part — amenable to purpose, to satisfaction and to participant society in and with it. Our logic then proposes that this situation is to be rightly interpreted in terms of inclusive purpose, satisfaction and responsibility. What means was 'meant to mean.' What evokes our response was responsibly so contrived. In a word it was created by a will that meant and made it so. We cannot categorically deny that we may be reading ourselves into it, nor prove that we are not. The atheist *may* be right that there is only us. But there is much sense in thinking that our experience of 'meant-ness' is derivative, sensing and assuming an inclusive one — a thesis certainly not capable of disproof and more commendable to sanity, humility and hope. Rather than seeing divine intention an illusion arising out of ours we may better understand the reality of ours issuing from the yet more real, the enveloping reality both ruling and risking creation.

Biblical faith, however, does not stay so to ruminate or postulate. It believes: 'In the beginning God created the heavens and the earth . . .' It proceeds to locate significance around the being of man, the creature in and over creation. Then rapidly it begins to focus on particular man, tribal man. Here lay its greatest demerit the correction of which was to be the travail and, as we will see, the achievement, of the Christhood of Jesus in the shape of the New Testament Church. That correction was the liberation out of ethnic and covenantal priority, into inclusively human openness, of the Messianic reality.

In the geographical awareness and historical perspective of those far-off days when the Hebrew editors and chroniclers were penning their Scriptures faith was instinctively self-centred. They saw the Creator's intention in terms of their own identity. Creation, they perceived, was for the sake of

Abraham. Their conviction was that all really began with his
call to inherit a land, a call for which the created world was
merely the arena. Revelation, then, starts with Chapter 12
of Genesis rather than Chapter 1. The natural is for the sake
of the historical and the historical hinges on the Hebraic.
So we have the patriarchs, inaugurators of 'the chosen seed'
and pilgrim-tenants of the proper territory.

In this way those perennial ingredients of all identity —
memory, birth and land — (who we are, where we are, whence
we are) came to comprise, for Hebrews, the elemental
intention of creation at large. This ethnic, historical,
territorial particularism was sanctioned and reinforced by
the saga of bondage in, and exodus from, the land of Egypt.
All three denominators of Hebrew-ness were fortified and
hallowed by that drama of tragedy and triumph. 'All our
fathers were under the cloud and all passed through the sea.'
It was the authentic proof of destiny. Then the wilderness
of Sinai and the covenant with Yahweh. However we understand the story it is the Hebraic sense of it which signifies.
Thence, via Joshua, the Judges, Samuel and Saul — seer and
king — to David with the possession of Jerusalem as both
means and symbol of the consolidation of all the tribes on
their destined land under a single sovereignty which was itself
to become a legend and a vision.

All this belongs with the Messianic idea in Israel. It spells
that which demands to be perpetuated through all generations. By the same token it stands for what is always prey to
jeopardy. For, despite every assumed warrant of divine will
and Hebrew right, the land had not been theirs by 'vacant
possession.' On the contrary, occupancy had necessitated
Joshua and David. There were the Philistines. The aftermath
of Exodus had generated tribal enmities of great ferocity.
'The Lord would be at war with Amalek from generation to
generation.' (Exodus 17.16) Edom and Moab were despoilers
on the way. Uneasily the people knew that what had been
forcibly acquired could be forcibly filched away. The Messianic vision — intriguingly recalled in John 1 with Nathaniel
'under the fig tree' symbol of the Messianic peace —
was of 'every man under his vine and under his fig-tree and
none shall make them afraid.' But precisely because vines

and fig-trees were equally desirable to erstwhile dwellers in their shade and benison, these former tenants might well covet and acquire them anew. Hence the wistful note of 'none shall make them afraid.' Messiah must be the supreme securer of their world, the means to confirm absolute validity by abiding safety.

Davidic monarchy could do this, while it endured. But beyond its fragmentation and demise there came at length the desolating exile, in which identity no longer enjoyed the very land itself. Both before and after that shattering climax of dismay came the prophets, keepers of the conscience, searchers of the corporate soul. The sense of compromise and sin's grim requital gave birth to visions of purity and hope, for which the heyday of 'the kingdom of our father David' might supply the pattern. Or memories of the good King Hezekiah might suggest the delineaments of the decisive future ruler, correcting aberration and bringing history back into the true. For, without such Messianic expectation, how could the intention of creation, staked as it was on Hebrew manhood and destiny, be loyal to the covenant which had sealed it? The liability of God must argue the retrieval of wayward history.

Memories and convictions ensured that the Messianic hope would have a royal quality, and that it would concern the national wellbeing, executing justice and attaining security for Israel. But the trauma of exile brought, with the great prophets who both preceded and accompanied it, different bearings and pre-occupations. Exile deepened the quandaries of the covenant, taking them beyond security only to survival itself. Recovery of the land remained central to vision of the future but what of the reality of suffering and what of the self-reproach and the evil that had merited its forfeiture? How was the divine design to be discerned when 'the day of the Lord was darkness, and not light'? Categories of the Messianic would have to embrace sterner reaches of wrong and perplexity than the ideal King could command.

Yet as the categories deepened, so also did the yearning. The more faith was cast upon the enigma of the divine the more it was required to wrestle with the Messianic clue. For, in the last analysis, Messiah would be the answer to the question set by history, the vindication of the covenant. If the land has been for the sake of the Temple as the focal point of its sanctity perhaps a priestly Messiah would fulfill what hope awaited. For it was Aaron who was first 'anointed' and there must needs be something 'priestly' about any figure Messianically anointed. But then was not 'priesthood' in a way collective, on behalf of all? Could it be that the community, the people of God as such, would be the instrument of His great design? If *they* had been elected, emancipated, enlandised, and even exiled, must not *they* be the corporate means to the final goal? Was it not said that if Israel were truly to keep one single Sabbath Messiah would arrive? Then the secret must lie in a people truly in Torah, disciplined, resolute and meticulous.

But all such thoughts of a Messiah-in-the-whole fell foul of the fact that it was almost the whole who were in the wrong. The thought, and doctrine, of 'the Remnant' so acknowledged. If hope were to be viable it must narrow, not enlarge, its agency. It was the nation that proved to be its own worst enemy, as the prophets saw it. How then could the nation, in apostacy, save itself from its own infidelity? Such thoughts only sharpened the dimensions of Messiah's task. No longer could it be assumed to mean the subduing of the nation's enemies, the unmasking of Gentile conspiracy, the ensuring of Hebraic right. Its sternest vocation would be with the people themselves, their inward wrongfulness, their domestic evils. How then were a compromised people to give rise, out of guilt and sin, to the means of their own redemption? What if 'the faithful remnant,' as with Jeremiah, were reduced almost to a single loyal soul?

It was in this context that we must set the mystery of 'the suffering servant' described by the second Isaiah, and ask of his identity and origins. Was 'the servant' the whole nation, idealised? Or a figure whose delineaments of pain and sorrow we can recognise in suffering prophets? We have already seen in chapter 1 how prophetic suffering enduring through and beyond tragedy was taken by the first Christians as the clue to Jesus. We have learned how, when tragic suffering was acknowledged as having been borne on behalf of the truth and had thus proved vicariously borne for the wrongdoers, how, further, by that realisation, the very wrongdoers could stand in the fruits of costly tragedy, and so be 'justified.' This emerged as the New Testament faith concerning where and how Messiah had truly come.

But such thoughts about Messianic actuality were almost, if not completely, absent from the pre-Christian scene. Despite how pointed the clue was in the experience of Jewry, the thought of reading the Messiah in the figure of 'the servant' was too remote from the rooted assumptions of power, too scandalous to satisfy the nation's pride, too anomalous to qualify as hope. When exile was repaired, Cyrus — as its sovereign repairer — became thereby 'God's servant.' Tenuous and precarious as return to the land of promise proved, it survived into the thrusting days of the Maccabees, whose martial ardour and strong arm seemed suited to salvation. *Magnificat* could then be credibly sung — as indeed it was by mothers of those warriors — more suitably than by a wistful Mary, or — should we say — an imaginative Luke by leave of her.?

There are many features of the Messianic theme through its long story variously debated by scholars, some of whom, in the complexities of conjecture and research, tend to minimise its importance or at least dispute its centrality. It is time to turn to how the theme bears on the ministry of Jesus and how that ministry came to be seen as its veritable fulfilment as the ground-plan of Christianity.

That 'the servant' of the Isaiah passages was understood by the early Church as prototype of the Messiah Jesus had been cannot be in serious doubt. The very language of those passages echoes through almost all the books of the New Testament, most notably the four Gospels and the First Epistle of Peter. With certain psalms in the same sense, they would seem to have been the very quarry from which the writers drew to set down both the narrative and the meaning of the Passion of Jesus. That, in itself, goes some way to sustain the belief that they had it so from Jesus himself. For they were, after all, interpreting what they had witnessed or 'reported.' Like the onlookers and 'reporters' in Isaiah 53, they both received and related what was utterly surprising in its implications and, therefore, no matter of

invention or conjecture on their own part. The root Christian theme of the 'tradition,' as that which becomes 'report'
from them only because it has been 'report' to them, is
precisely how it had been centuries before with the 'repute'
of 'the servant.'

But it is necessary, for honesty's sake, to press enquiry
further and ask of the evidence that Jesus himself was
consciously identifying the Messianic task with the servant
'image' and both with himself. The surest way to do this,
through the tangled debates and arguments of a long and
laboured scholarship, is to focus on the fact of hostility and
rejection which, in growing intensity, circumstantially
placed Jesus in the context of 'the servant' precedent, and
further to ask what he did, in point of fact, with that actuality.
For, emphatically, it was of a kind to pose for him the burden
of a situation for which there was no clearer parallel than
that mysteriously present in the Isaiah text. Whether or not
response and vocation were on the same model, what
necessitated and might evoke them certainly was.

There is, however, a prior need to study how it was that
the situation of hostility and tragedy supervened within
his ministry and how the clear Messianic motif became
suffused with suffering. On the face of it, resistance would
seem to be the unlikeliest attitude to the message Jesus
brought. Who would want to quarrel with the Beatitudes or
dispute the sanity and simplicity of the parables? The 'elder
brother' in the story of the wandering son might refuse to
share rejoicing at the wayward one's return, but surely every
hearer must have hoped he would. And what could prompt
antagonism to the healing of the leprous and the re-sighting
of the blind? At the outset, when we are with the Synoptic
Gospels in Galilee all seems springlike and promising around
the personality of Jesus — apart, that is, from certain local
difficulties at Nazareth.

Yet Galilee, with its cosmopolitan folk of mixed races and
its harp-shaped lake and gentle music, was not the whole
story. There was Jerusalem, walled around and rugged, a
bastion of other forces. And Jesus, it seems, was inexorably
drawn there as to the ultimate stronghold of what he must
engage. For in his message he was transmuting some of the

dearest cherished elements in the Judaic tradition in which
he stood. His preaching was bewilderingly transforming the
question of God. He loved what grammarians have called
'the divine passive', the Aramaic usage: 'My son, there is One
who forgives your sins', 'There is One who has numbered
all the hairs of your head', 'There is One who comforts those
who mourn.' Some hundred times we find that Aramaic form
of speech. The reality of God belongs with the living
present, in ready forgiveness, in insistent compassion, in
dealings not confined to the already 'righteous' but open
to the broken and the lost. God is more than the other pole
of chosen peoplehood: His love, like His rain, comes upon
'the just and the unjust alike.'

This 'new wine' burst out of the 'old wineskins' of a
meticulous law. It penetrated to pollution within, not
merely without, and it presumed to override the ritual law
in the obligations of the moral law. Thus it challened, while
it honoured, the supremacy of the Sabbath, understanding
the sacred day as 'made for man.' Indeed, man was made for
Sabbaths, fitted for the rest and perspective they bring and
needing their sacrament of divine claim, but not at the
expense of love and neighbour.

Such awareness of the pitfalls of piety and the limits of
ritual religion made possible a new attitude to outsiders and
the 'fallen', an attitude which Jesus steadily practised in deed
as well as word. The expectation of the dispirited was
quickened by hearsay of him and wistful taxgatherers might
climb into concealing sycamores to see him pass beneath
— or a Samaritan woman of dubious history be startled
into conversation in his presence. There was a climate of
hope within the conviction that 'the kingdom of God' was
actual and present, 'in the midst', and not remote in future
judgement or lost in the backward mists of memory.

Throughout in what we may perhaps call 'Jesus' theism'
there ran an assurance, a note of authority, not pretentious
but effectual. His own 'society with sinners' had within it the
confidence that it was even so with God. Indeed, the divine
original underlay the earthly actual and both obtained within
his own person and his own consciousness. 'I am come . . .'
he would say: Or: 'the Son of Man is come . . .' using a loved

form of phrase in which a significance displaces the personal pronoun. In this way we have to conclude that in some sense there was — in his ministry — an interplay between 'the kingdom of God' and the identity of Jesus. The one evidenced itself in the other, the other expressed and realised the nature of the one. In believing so, we are pondering what Jesus must have been like to have elicited what his disciples came to believe him to have been.

But that ultimate discovery awaited the Resurrection. It could only come on the further side of the climax to which such ministry moved in our sort of world. The impact of Jesus on the time and the place headed into tragedy. For in all its features it was in radical contention with the institutions of his day precisely because of his identity with them. He was no stranger to temple and synagogue, no alien from the loved tradition of Moses and David and the prophets. We do not rightly understand Jesus as some 'Gentile' intrusion into the heritage of Abraham. The theme of 'Jesus the Jew' — and indeed, later, 'those Jews the apostles' — is entirely authentic. It was the mission and the message from within that aroused the unease from within, and all of it symptomatic of the perverse potential of *all* traditions and collective identities in the human scene.

The several notes of the ministry of Jesus generated the rejection he underwent at institutional hands. The Sabbath had to be protected from the inroads of a libertarian pleading his own conscience. The moral law would be safe only in the inviolability of the ritual law. If there were to be an equal mercy on the part of God for prostitutes and quislings how would the integrity of the righteous be recognised and rewarded? Could there be any such immediacy of authority of the kind to which Jesus confidently laid claim? If there were to be, what then of the pointlessness of all things traditional, official and respectable? Such alleged intimacy with the divine conspired against all that was appropriate to the collective consciousness of the people of God through their legitimate organs of covenant and scripture.

Nor was the instinct for rejection only religious. The Sadducean mind found a charismatic leader of Jesus' style an implicit menace to the status quo, disruptive of the delicate balance of relationship with Rome. To the Zealot mind such a 'populist' — unless he could be recruited and suborned — was worse than useless, could serve no ends in the rugged violence with which Messiah must stain his hands. On every count political, the omens darkened over Jesus' brief career. Galilee was leading to Gethsemane. When Luke writes of 'the Scribes and Pharisees' 'murmuring' his language suggests the distant rumbling of the thunder and the gathering storm.

In that passage, and indeed everywhere, the latent quarrel authority had with Jesus only evoked his teaching the more clearly. The parable of the lost sheep, silver and son, followed the murmuring in the evangelist's account. The last parable, in its conclusion, deliberately, pointedly, captured the mood which occasioned it in the one who was self-exempted from the celebration. A further parable of the husbandmen and the vineyard only deepened the confrontation with its use of cherished Hebraic imagery and its clear implication from the logic of rejected prophets. It can hardly have had place in Jesus' public teaching without being also a telling insight into the tragic destiny awaiting 'sonship' to the vineyard's Lord.

Could we, then, be on surer ground than in locating the Messianic issue in this living context of 'the gathering storm.'? The teaching and the ministry had indeed been 'messianic' in their delineation of the character of 'the kingdom of heaven' present and active in society. But the very reception of those tokens, paradoxically, had kindled a response which measured the reach of human wrongness and, so doing, reached the final measure of Messiah's task. Certainly we find the writers of the four Gospels focussing on the factors leading to a decision on the part of Jesus that in suffering what rejection would entail lay the Messianic meaning.

'Whom do men say that I am?' he asked his disciples, according to Matthew, Mark and Luke, and, further, 'Whom do you say that I am?' We cannot intelligently read this as other than an inner wrestling with a sense of destiny. (It is not some omniscience pretending to need information). The point in the story is presented by the evangelists as a clear

turning-point. We must understand a Jesus feeling his way
to decision in fellowship — remote and inadequate it is
true — with intimate associates. 'From that time on' Jesus
began to educate them into the implications, so distant from
their dreams, which the Messiahship they had recognised
must — in Jesus' terms — entail.

If we rightly see Jesus sustained in Messianic decision by
the logic of what his own ministry experienced from its
human context, it is because that experience takes us — as
it took him — into the full extent of what requires
Messiahship, namely the evil disposition of our human
nature in wilful self-esteem and collective pride. That is the
realism and the honesty of the Gospel. The Messiah has to
be defined by where the role leads. It leads to Calvary. In
comprehending a 'Christ-shaped story' we are not only
tracing the framework of an ancient hope: we are identifying its fulfilment in the self-giving of 'the man of sorrows.'

From the turning point of that story the decision moves
steadily into crisis. Everything at stake takes on a sharper
tone. Jesus' tenacity of purpose is answered by accentuated
rejection and a hardening of the will. The narrative of the
ministry passes into the climax of the Passion. The Passover
meal gives form to the memorialising of the Cross. Judas,
presumably despairing of an activist Messianism, enters
into conspiracy with the authorities and receives his retaining fee. The other disciples, disallowed the only form of
loyalty they understand, are broken in despair. Jesus undertakes to 'suffer the contradiction of sinners' and, so doing,
achieves the Messianic vocation by his own interpretation
of its demands. The achievement crowned the ministry which,
by virtue of the sonship of Jesus to the Father, had yielded
the clue so long awaited and so long elusive. The ministry,
we may say, had been at odds with human wilfulness in its
most elemental subtlety. The message, in its very un-
wantedness, had disclosed the human heart. Messiah had
become so, by undertaking in the Cross the consequences
of our being the humanity we are. His teaching and his
suffering were one inclusive whole at grips, by word and deed,
with the wrongness of the world and out of the encounter
fashioning the Messianic fact, 'the kingdom of heaven'

inseparably one with this 'kingship.'

Perhaps this open secret is nowhere more tersely drama-tised than in the way the Fourth Gospel narrates the appearance of Jesus before Pilate's judgement seat.

> 'Are you the king of the Jews?'
> 'Are you using this word, Pilate, as you would as a Roman, or is it a word others have used in telling about me?'
> 'Am I a Jew?' It is your own nation and the chief priests who have brought you here before me. What have you done?'
> 'My kingdom is not of the kind you have in mind, a kingdom in this world. Were it so, my servants would not have let me get into the hands of the Jewish authorities: they would have fought. But my kingdom is not of that sort.'
> 'So you are a king then?'
> 'King' is the word you're using. I was born and I came into the world with one end in view — to bear witness to the truth. Those who are of the truth, they listen.'
> 'What is truth?'

Pilate went out, 'jesting,' it was said, 'not staying for an answer.' From the same climax, and by a different 'judgement' the Church went out not staying to delay the answer: 'God has made this Jesus Lord and Christ.'

Doubtless there have been, and will continue to be, differing versions, from scholars and critics, of what was enigma to Pilate and remains enigma to them. The Chris-tian conviction does not stand in need of timid immunity from all contrary suggestion, some of which we will review in chapter 6. The act of recognition, which Christian faith made, knows itself as a decision and believes it to have been right. But decision it remains in a context for which other options are not to be suppressed. On the contrary, a fair exploration of them will be part of the honesty of the continuing decision. The Church lived, and only lived, in the faith that it had rightly recognised what was authentically recognisable in Jesus crucified, namely the eternal design within the Messianic meaning. For Jesus had encountered within his own preaching what the travail of that meaning was. The travail undertaken had, therefore, translated hope into act and concept into deed. In this way there is an essential unity between the Gospel *of* Jesus in what he taught and the Gospel *about* Jesus as it came to be in the teaching of the Church.

We have, then, to pass to the third aspect of 'the Christ-shaped story,' from the antecedents in Jewry and achievement in Jesus, to affirmation by the disciples. There can be no doubt about how dramatic and forthright the affirmation was. It has been a long pre-occupation of New Testament students to suspect that when the Gospels took shape their image of Jesus was no longer original. It had been conformed to later belief, apart, perhaps, from certain tell-tale details which escaped the process. The merits of that case concern us later. What is clear, in any event, is that the writing enshrined a verdict, that it told a conviction in the shape of a story. In that sense, whatever calls the New Testament into question confirms it. It can hardly be suspected of a *parti pris* and be denied as witnessing to a conviction. It has always been more intelligent to think the conviction warranted by the story than to see the story warped by the conviction. If the 'original' in Jesus was not as faith enshrined it in its literature it is hard to know where faith or literature originated.

As we have seen in chapter 1, the Resurrection was the crucial factor in faith-origination — but not resurrection as some anomalous wonder, only Resurrection as the point of realisation of the truth, the sign of Messianic fact. It falls to chapter 3 to explore carefully how 'the Christ-telling faith' proceeded from that inauguration. Here it will be illuminating to go at once to the narrative of Saul/Paul's experience on the road to Damascus, even at the risk of seeming to incur the charge that Paul entails misgivings — a charge we would repudiate. For there is a sense in which his 'conversion' embraces — drama apart — what New Testament conversion means. And there are other, fascinating features of the story which serve our exposition well.

We start with Messianic community, with a group of men and women witnessing, first in Jerusalem and then in dispersion, to Jesus as Messiah and Messiah in Jesus. This incurs resistance — a resistance in line with that experienced by Jesus but now, for obvious reasons, intensified. We have the beginnings already of the concept of 'the body of Christ,' a peoplehood carrying on his meaning and in some sense reproducing the Messianic principle of suffering for truth. It is a community which sees itself perpetuating not only the memory but the actuality of Jesus and his Cross. Indeed, the actuality takes memory itself into trust — which is the way of the risen Christ.

At the heart of Saul's vision on the road is this identity between Jesus and community. The voice demanded of Saul: 'Why are you persecuting me?' and then, responding to Saul's dazed question, declared: 'I am Jesus whom you persecute.' A voice from heaven saying: 'I am the Christ' might have fascinated any pious Jew, but not surprised him. For was not 'the Christ' assumed to 'ride on clouds of power.'? What was significant was that *Jesus* held that place. *Where* the voice spoke from signified to *whom* the voice belonged — to Jesus Christ. Here, from beginning to end, is the index to Paul's career and theology, a sustained 'obedience to the heavenly vision.'

It is right to read here, as in epitome, all the elements present in the New Testament Epistles. Jesus crucified as Christ and Lord, a solidarity with him in witness and in suffering, community born of solidarity, a unity in Christ ready to incorporate on the sole condition of faith, a readiness to address the arch-persecutor as 'brother Saul.' These together embody the meaning of the Resurrection, the living continuity of the Christ within the vicissitudes of the world — vicissitudes which are to be read in the light of the precedent by which Jesus had responded to his experience in the world. That precedent is known and felt, not as an abstract recollection, but as an energising presence mysteriously enabling its own reproduction. This enabling comes to be enshrined in the doctrine of the Holy Spirit, as the abiding self of Jesus enthusing and indwelling 'the church which is his body.'

That sense of things was under no illusion that somehow the Messianic in Jesus had left no redeeming room for them. He had forever disclosed what redeeming the world would take and left the legacy to them. But they would more surely bears its sorrows and overcome its evils by the knowledge that the inclusive event had happened which equipped them to do so by its gift of forgiveness and its mandate of peace with God. Paul believed intensely that 'the heavenly vision' had made good his non-participation in the actual ministry of Jesus and so qualified him, alongside such participants, to be an apostle. That conviction, on his part, may be read as a sign of the inherent unity between Jesus being the Christ in the story and Jesus being the Christ in the awareness of the Church. But that same sequence of event into experience, of fact into recognition, dominates the entire literature of the apostles.

It was this unity of the story with the decision which underlay the whole pattern of New Testament authority, the authority which became a necessity of growth and expansion and of the discipline these made vital. To be 'apostolic' meant knowledge of the living Jesus of Nazareth *and* his acknowledgement as the Christ of God. The credentials of authority stood in both knowledge and acknowledgement. Hence Paul's insistence, in writing to the Galatians and elsewhere, that he qualified on both counts. It is fair to say that the crux of the question of apostolic authority was the concern that the shape of Christ should continue to control both faith and fellowship. When vexing tensions arose — as inevitably they did in the vagaries of time and the stresses of human nature — having companied with Jesus and awareness of the Christ together constituted apostolic integrity. How it proceeded belongs with chapter 3.

Meanwhile, there is one dimension of the Christ-shaped story which, thus far, we have deliberately deferred, namely the 'sonship' of Jesus. The question is often posed: 'Did Jesus actually claim to be 'the Son of God'?' The question is not well put, if by 'claimed' we mean some abstract, formal pretension. From all we have studied, it is wiser to say that he sensed it or, better, that he lived it. For it was the meaning of what earlier we called Jesus' theism. The word 'Father,' and that in the tenderest terms, was his instinctive, habitual address to God. The vocation implicit in a suffering Messiahship he sensed as being 'the cup my Father has given me.' 'Our Father' was the word he taught his disciples as the plea to open prayer. His own 'sonship' consisted in his entire responsiveness, his sense of intimacy, his partnership in will, his confidence in purpose, his awareness of mission. How it was to be understood to 'consist', in status and the language of later Christology, was the task of theology in the sequel. But all those efforts after definition, within the categories congenial to those who made them, had to do with how veritable, how authentic, the active sonship was. The way in which Jesus was the Christ, implementing the mind of God in being so, is what this sonship means and remains the concern of doctrine when it passes from the historical to the conceptual, from what was known in deed to what is told in thought.

Our surest reliance here will be in the theme of obedience, so prominent in the Passion narratives and in the pastoral education *via* the Epistles. Clearly in what is denoted by 'obedience' in any context there are two poles. There is that which requires to be obeyed and there is the response doing so. Obedience, like allegiance, is rendered where it is awaited. All that we have been studying about the pattern of the Christ in the story is, therefore, an index to the nature of God. For all was guided, sustained and accomplished in the faith that the Father so willed. We only have the Christ as he was in apprehending the Father as He is. When, later, theologians talked of 'the pre-existent Christ' what, in part, they had in mind was simply the eternal nature of God historically discerned by men in the action of Jesus in his Christhood. Or, as the Gospels expressed it: 'He that has the Son has the Father also.' If our whole emphasis in this book, mirrored in the very title chapters, seems to be pre-occupied with 'Christ,' it is only because he is the context of our pre-occupation with God. If we come to God through Jesus it is only in that we have Jesus as he was because of God. Whether in the story or in the worship we are within the one circle of love.

In the language of the evangelists it is this harmony of purpose which is expressed in the words addressed to, or about, Jesus at the baptism and the transfiguration: 'This is my Son, my beloved, in whom is My pleasure.' It is a salutation which may be thought to combine the royal sonship ascribed to David and to corporate Israel, with the 'loved-ness' of the servant in the Isaiah passages. In that event the Gospels are affirming exactly that identification of the

'son' with the 'servant' which we have taken throughout to
have been the mind of Jesus. The meaning is not some benign
bestowal of favour or attitude of external approval in some
static way. Rather it has to do with a mind sharing God's mind,
thinking as God thinks, making an active union of wills, the
one designing the other achieving the single objective. This
mutuality, eternal, incarnational, is the meaning of the loved-
ness responsively to love that belong together in the
Messiahship of Jesus. The faith about Jesus was the Gospel
about God. The story, on both counts, intended the world.

CHAPTER 3

The Christ-telling Faith

Many and varied titles have been ascribed to Jesus. 'Jesus the writer' is not among them. Yet, from the time of the Fourth Gospel, 'the Word' has been among the most dearly treasured. Jesus left no documents: his teaching was always oral. All he had said and meant lay in the minds and hearts of men and women of his company. At the close of the Gospels we are left only with people, with a band of disciples 'returning to Jerusalem.' They were all there was.

And they proved to be all that was necessary. It was from them that scriptures came, or from the pens of those whom they recruited. 'The Christ-shaped story' we have traced was first told in lives and only then in script. These were the twin, inter-acting consequences of the fact of Jesus — community and record. As 'the Word made flesh' he passed on into history by a society of the faithful and by their writing of the faith. The New Testament as literature derives from its people: its people belong in the New Testament as its *raison d'être*. These, together, enshrine our whole study in the decision that decided Christianity. Made about Jesus as Lord and Christ, it was made good in folk and made plain in Gospels and Epistles recording both him and them. What is now our concern is the decision in its literature.

Dramatic their discovery of faith was: but it was also cumulative. For by its own momentum it took them out into reaches of time and place and circumstance into which it had to be translated and fulfilled. The faith's intention for the world meant new dimensions of culture and language, from the Aramaic of Jesus to the Greek of the Mediterra-nean scene, from the familiar assumptions of Judaic tradition to the mental and social order in the Graeco-Roman world. It is true that Jew and Greek had already in dispersion partially assimilated each other's heritage but in no way suiting the scandal of a faith about a cross. That new faith was destined to encounter scepticism or ostracism from many sides and to wrestle with communication in a welter of contradiction. Jewish themes and Greek vocabulary — not to say Roman roads and Roman cities — might serve its passage into its world vocation, but only by strenuous ventures both of travel and of travail.

Receding time meant new generations replacing those who had known 'the Word made flesh.' Original disciples might be scattered far in the dispersion but mortality steadily thinned their ranks. There is an interesting note in passing when Luke's narrative of Paul's transit through Caesarea en route to Jerusalem tells of their lodging with 'Mnason, a Cypriot' and 'an old disciple.' (Acts 21.16). As such survivors became rarer, the more urgent became the need to set down from memory into writing the themes and deeds of Jesus. Lapsing years were no less a spur to record than the extending reach of mission. Both were to present the churches with tests of character and conviction as the faith made its way through untried issues like circumcision, idolatry, partisanship and ecstatic enthusiasms, where a loyalty to Jesus needed to be discerned.

The story of the forming of the Gospel tradition is complex and in part controversial, and its detailed study exacting. Overall, we may say that we have memory informing the future and its future re-forming the memory. There is a clear bifocal quality in all the four Gospels, so that the setting of the churches bears upon the telling of their origin in Jesus. It is vital to appreciate this fundamental situation and to register how it might be likened to the notes of a single chord, or the double sense of an irony but without the wry intent of ironists. Situations confronting new Christians in the wider world are illuminated by the retrospect to Galilee and Gethsemane and retrospect, in turn, is coloured by situations into which its meanings are translated.

This is not to say that 'situational' composition of the Gospels falsifies their rendition of Jesus. While it is true that we have no documentation of him apart from Christian portrayal (though careful scholars seek to make good this state of things by inference from other sources, not always rightly aligned in time), the basic confidence remains in the fact that, by experience and obedience, they were best qualified to know. If we see what they were as being con-sequential to what he was, then there can be no surer presentation. But that sort of reliance on them involves — and readily concedes — that theirs was a partiality in the describing of him, a partiality which nothing external to experience such as theirs would be competent to correct, and where, in the nature of things 'impartiality' would be devoid of the data only commitment possessed.

In a passage, earlier noted, at the end of his *The Quest of the Historical Jesus,* Albert Schweitzer, in his belief that the 'quest' had a disconcerting inconclusiveness, saw Jesus 'coming to us as one unknown,' or most certainly *not* as known in orthodox Christianity. Nevertheless, so coming in that 'unknown-ness' for historians, Jesus could yet be known by us 'in the toils, the conflicts, the sufferings which (we) shall pass through in his fellowship . . . in the tasks which he has for us to fulfill for our time.' The confidence, if not the unknown-ness, was well and finely stated. It seems strange, however, that Schweitzer should have distrusted the New Testament's own 'known-ness' of Jesus in just such toils, conflicts and sufferings' in that first generation of those who followed him. For it is precisely such knowing which the New Testament records and without which it would not exist.

It is important for us in reckoning with this shape of things in the New Testament to ponder the distinction between facts and truths. For we live in a climate of mind for which only facts are truths, whereas there are innumerable facts which do not constitute truths. Those familiar with the English Civil War and its sequel in the 17th century, will know as a fact that Charles 1st, the King of England, lost his head in January, 1649. But that fact is far from being the truth of what some saw as a martyrdom by regicides, and others saw as a verdict against absolutism altering the course of English history. The fact of the matter in the Book of Exodus is that Mount Sinai was volcanic and in eruption at the time of Moses. That fact is far short of the truth of the covenant-drama dominating the long story of Hebraic self-awareness. When the young

Satyamuni, the Buddha to be, left the princely palace, in point
of fact he saw a sick man, an old man and a corpse. He
believed he saw the essential truth of mortal futility attaching
to transience.

Examples of this vital distinction between fact and truth
are legion. Reality has to be fully stated and statements that
neglect meaning impoverish even their facts. At best they
might be likened to a song that is only read, at worst to a
clock without a face. This sense of a sad reductionism, even
of a deceptiveness, in mere fact does not mean that all
confidence about attaining to the truth within a fact is
justified. On the contrary truth-readings *may* distort fact-
situations. But the remedy then is not to suppose the
reductionism is all there is, but to pursue the latent clues
more wisely. The best credentials in so doing are likely to
be those most germane to what is at stake and most intimate
with its relevance. It is just such 'likeliness' which, we can
be soberly confident, characterises the New Testament in the
fact-truth equation concerning Jesus as the Christ. It was not
simply saying what the song was, it was singing it.

What is at issue here might be suggested — if the analogy
is not wrongly pressed — by thought of a tree as roots and
branches. The tree is one, and grows from and because of
its roots. But those roots necessarily grow also with the growth
above ground. As the derivative above enlarges and extends
so, commensurately, the source below deepens and solidifies.
In a comparable sense the documentation of Jesus takes off
from its roots in his story but lets them partake in the life
of what they grew into. To have this tree metaphor, and to
have it in proper discipline, is to understand the relation
between story and faith, between history and theology,
obtaining in all the Gospels and in John's most of all.
Examples of the relation will best come after some brief
review of Gospel formation.

A feature which at once presents itself in Matthew, as the
first Gospel in actual order and which occurs less obtrusively
in them all, is the concern of the evangelists to link their
narrative with precedent in the prophets. They had an
instinctive sense of the relevance of the past as foreshowing
what had eventuated. With that sense went a certain

urgency for the support such retrospect afforded. The
urgency lay in the disconcerting, even scandalous, nature of
the message they brought. A crucified Messiah embracing
Jew and Gentile alike — those were the two utterly un-
congenial themes in their story. 'Who could believe our
report?' Isaiah 53.1 had asked, 'who will ever credit what has
come to our knowledge and we are now telling?' 'The man
of sorrows' then had been a matter of incredulity, tidings
of whom had been as 'despised and rejected' as the one they
commended. The Church knew it the same with the message
of Jesus as the crucified Christ, while the impulse to share
that identity with all and sundry and, so doing, propose to
incorporate them into one community in Christ was
equally incredible.

In this situation which — as is clear notably in John —
only intensified as the new faith matured, it was natural that
the evangelists set great store by corroboration from the
Scriptures which were so central to the allegiance of their
Jewish readers. It is true that John has Jesus deploring how
such readers were 'searching the Scriptures' while refusing
him. But that is only a measure of how controversy tended
to take the form of conflict over texts. When people are
at odds about the substance they will be at odds about
the sources. Controversy apart, the apostles sought the
confirmation old writings could yield for them in the task
of telling their faith and justifying the range of their
fellowship.

So far did this seeking go that some scholars have suspected
that things happened in the record's perspective *because* they
had happened in the precedent perceived as belonging to
them. It would not be wrong, or sceptical, in some cases at
least, to think so. Matthew and Luke (only) locate the birth
of Jesus in Bethlehem. Researchers question whether they
were right. But whatever that 'fact' — to revert to our earlier
distinction — the 'truth' was that they knew him as 'the son
of David' and the prophet Micah, knowing Bethlehem as
David's birthplace, saw the place as being the natal ground
of the leader yet unborn. Bethlehem, then, for Matthew and
Luke, was the geographical counterpart of the essential truth
about the Jesus they proclaimed. Matthew, likewise, takes the

holy family down to Egypt, through another Joseph, to bring
them up again to Messianic destiny. It is not the 'fact' —
which conjecture might dispute — that of itself, or alone,
sustains the 'truth': it is the latter which explains the former.
'Out of Egypt I called My son.'

Matthew again, though the most Hebrew-minded of the
four in his citations from the Old Testament, alone brings
the Magi from 'the east.' Isaiah 60.1-3 had given noble
expression to the universal magnetism of Jerusalem's Lord
and seen the nations coming to his light, bringing gold and
incense. The evangelist finds both comfort and anticipation
in the vision of old and, knowing the fulfilment in one
crucified, adds myrrh to gold and incense. Is he not finely
corroborating what he knows of Jesus and the Gentiles in
the imagery of prophetic foresight? That being the truth of
his narrative we would be dull not to let it take care of the
facts.

What, further, of Luke's *Magnificat* and the other hymnology with which he opens his Gospel and which have a
Hebraic feel quite different from the rest of his writing?
Indeed, his Gospel seems to begin again at 3.1, when the
songs end, 'in the fifteenth year of Tiberius Caesar.' Nowhere
in the New Testament is inspired, conscious composition so
imaginatively right, right, that is, from the churches'
retrospect. Where, we may well ask, did *Magnificat* come
from? How did Luke know what 'Mary sang' those x years
earlier when Luke was no more than an infant in arms or
dreaming of medicine as a calling? 'Facticians' may remind us
that Luke and Mary may have crossed paths in Ephesus, or
that tradition about the Nativity circulated where Luke
travelled with Paul. They may well be right. But such chances
do not explain why Luke chose as he did when he took up
his pen to write. The words were not his own, the inspired
employment of paradox was.

The *Magnificat* has clear echoes of the song of Hannah
in 1 Samuel 2. But it has even more intriguing association
with the Maccabees, those martial warriors and saviours of
Israel in the period prior to the yoke of Rome. They, or their
mothers, had sung the overthrow of the Seleucids, when,
indeed, 'the mighty were dethroned and the proud scattered.'

To have birth is the first requisite of all liberators. Luke sees
Mary's vocation as the mother of the Lord reversing martial
liberation the more pointedly by borrowing its language, and
exalting 'the humble and the meek' in the meaning of the
Gospel. What has happened in Jesus 'fills the hungry with
good things' and spells how God 'remembers His mercy.' The
evangelist finds confirmation in the words of Hebraic
tradition but the meaning he gives to them is all his own,
yet only so because of the truth of Jesus. Luke is no reporter
overhearing singing: he is a poet interpreting a truth.

There is the same sense of precedent in the Gospel
portrayal of John the Baptist. Perhaps some of the details
of his character and message are derived from the role the
forerunner fulfills in the prophetic expectation. But it
becomes legitimate as such because of what, at the time of
writing, had already ensued in Jesus as the Christ. Citation
of Scripture belongs with realisation of how its contents have
actually transpired in Jesus. It can then be recruited for the
description, the confirmation and the commendation of
belief in him. The case from precedent might have weight
with the dubious or the perplexed: it certainly had force for
the witnesses.

Nowhere is this feature of the Gospels writing their case
out of the Hebraic past more striking than in the final
chapter of Luke. The two disciples on the road to Emmaus,
and later the whole band in the upper room, are portrayed
as experiencing this 'scriptured-ness' of Jesus as the meaning of the Resurrection itself. Luke sees the two travellers
as discussing animatedly the failure of their hopes and the
agonising tragedy of what had happened to Jesus. Jesus comes
alongside, reaching the inn in their company and sharing
their meal. Luke understands him 'expounding in all the
Scriptures things concerning himself.' That phrasing has
aroused in some quarters an over-inventiveness with
typology. It surely means a consensus, a logic, of the whole,
tending — as we saw in the previous chapter — to the Christ
as indispensable to history, given creation and covenant, and
the Cross as inseparable from the Christ. The entire Gospel,
the being of the Church, hinge on that consensus. Scripture,
Luke avows, intends and undergirds them both.

But all is as paradoxical as the *Magnificat*. It is just that
Christian paradox, the kingship of the love that suffers, which
needs, and finds, the consensus of all realist reckoning with
evil that history affords. Such is the burden, and the conviction, of Luke's authorship in this crowning passage so loved
down the centuries. 'The breaking of the bread' makes the
fellowship of the ages complete.

That suffering alone was the prelude to 'glory,' as in the
Lukan narrative, was central to Christian conviction. It is no
surprise, then, that the writing of the Passion should have
drawn upon words and glimpses present in earlier occasions
of travail, notably Psalm 22 with its detail uncannily close
to that of the crucifixion. If the evangelists drew upon the
psalm in their telling of the memory that would simply be,
on the narrative level, their perception of its meaning in the
same context of costly fidelity. To have readers perceive the
affinity between the Cross and the precedent was an inclusive
concern of the Gospel record, The convergence of detail is
a secondary, if striking, factor.

Matthew's authorship suggests that he had close to his
mind, if not his pen, a collection of texts seen, or believed,
to have been borne out in what had happened in the case
of Jesus. He was evidently moved also by *argumenta ad homines,*
in presentation calculated to address the mentality he encountered. For he clearly constructs his account of Jesus'
ministry around the parallel of Moses. There are twelve
disciples to correspond with the twelve tribes. Jesus' teaching
is gathered into a compendium delivered from a mountain,
as the new law of the kingdom. This setting helps to rein-
force the authority of: 'You have heard that it was said, but
I say to you ...' 'That it might be fulfilled ...' is one of his
favourite refrains. Though fulfilment is radical it nevertheless
cares for citations which may illuminate and commend it.

Reference to some possible hand-list of texts from the old
order as notes for the evangelists serves to remind the
student of Gospel formation that there were other sources
behind the existing Gospels which underlay them at an
embryonic stage. This much is clear from the common
material in all three 'Synoptic' (or unified view) Gospels,
Matthew, Mark and Luke. Scholars have noted how some

ninety per cent of Mark is present (not quite verbatim) in
Matthew, and some fifty per cent of him in Luke. But both
draw also on what has been assumed to be another source,
external to Mark, while Luke has material — very precious
in its quality — unique to himself. Given this situation,
within a broadly synoptic writing, it seems logical to
assume that oral memory had distilled into textual forms
available to all three, in part or in whole, as quarry for their
building. It must be assumed that this took shape in a
variety of locations with their immediate circumstances of
community life and apostolic association.

We must place it also in the context of the world revealed
in the Epistles, a world of continuing outreach and of
communal self-definition *vis-à-vis* the issues set by the
society around, the synagogues of the Jewish people, the idol
shrines of Graeco-Roman folk, the porches and academies
of the learned and even the kitchens of Caesar's household.
The founding fathers were accustomed to scriptures read
in their worship and to midrash, or exposition, based on the
oral Torah. It seems likely that as rehearsal of the words and
events of Jesus solidified into textual shape, readings in
assembly became the norm, with commentary on core texts
on the part of teachers and elders. It seems clear from the
modern study, known as form criticism, that some of this
Christian midrash on the parables of Jesus survived into the
corpus of Gospel writing. Such, at least, has been deduced
from meticulous comparison of the Gospels and the nuances
of each in the transmission of the same pericope, or passage.

It can be conjectured, but with no certainty, that such
liturgical or communal use of what became Gospel material
was affected by calendar sequence, instruction of the young
and of new adherents, and celebratory events. The retentive-
ness of memory slowly yielded its role to the fluidity of text,
and text yielded into the authorship and consolidation of
what we now possess as Gospels. But that whole sequence,
its fascinating detail beyond our certain reach, proceeds from
its fount in Jesus and its channel in community. The
present texts, for all the massive scholarship they have
received, are the work of Christ-telling faith.

The stage represented by the authorship, to which the

familiar phrase 'the Gospel according to . . .' belongs, was
undoubtedly one of deliberate editorial intent and literary
skill. The evangelists were the servants of their sources but
also their masters. They brought their own devotion and
perception to bear on their task, as noted already in Luke's
use of Nativity hymnology and Matthew's structure of the
ordered Sermon. The throb of urgency which Mark gives to
his narrative, carrying action forward with insistent speed,
like the very 'hound of heaven,' reveals how totally he is caught
up in what he tells. All the evangelists know that the Passion
is the climax and they move towards it with a vivid sense of
drama. In no way are they constructing a biography. Their
Gospels do not fit at all that genre of writing. They know
themselves on a *via crucis* and, like Paul's friends meeting
and escorting Paul on the Appian Way to the capital, they
bring Jesus through the road of ministry to the rendezvous
in the garden. It is an authorship, from within community,
which intends to relive — and have us all relive — what
decided Christianity.

Nowhere is this unique character of literature, the genre
of 'Gospel,' more arresting and, for some, more perplexing
than the Gospel of John. Nowhere is the context of the
writing more germane to what is written. John of Ephesus
is perhaps the best way to denote the author, thus
distinguishing him from numerous other Johns like the
Baptist and the son of Zebedee, brother of James, or the other
evangelist John Mark. The Gospel itself does not carry the
name of John. A final redactor, in chapter 21 (also called
John), ascribes the whole to 'the disciple whom Jesus loved,'
(as a repeated phrase has it), who may well have been a
Jerusalemite and a late recruit to Jesus, and who became in
old age the loved leader of a Johannine community in
the Ephesus region. It was this community's trials and
controversies which underlie the writer's presentation of the
Jesus he knew. For while he writes from long retrospect and
with the hindsight of lapsing years, he has the vivid, intimate
detail of an eye-witness. That quality blends remarkably with
the freedom of creative writing yielding, not a chronicle but
an interpretation.

Pastoral leadership in a vital centre of the faith and prolonged mature rumination on its origins in the person and the work of Jesus as the Christ are the marks of evangelist John. His writing bridges Palestine to Greek Asia and the years of event to the years of exposition. It interprets the Hebraic Messianic meaning into the ethos of the Mediterranean culture. Its Prologue (1.1-18) answers in the latter's idiom the question central to the former: 'Whom do you say that I am?' It does so successfully enough to have been mistaken by some critics for a 'gnostic' Gospel (though others have read it as 'anti-gnostic'). That puzzlement is evidence that its authentic Palestinianism is mediated into the thought-world of those whose vocabulary abounded in 'spiritual' terms, such as 'knowledge', 'light', 'truth', and 'sign'. John's uncompromising affirmation of 'the Word *made flesh*' countered, once and for all, the theosophies of the day, while presenting to them the Incarnation as 'the mystery of Christ'.

It is this quality in the portrayal which explains the contrast, so often noticed, between Jesus in John and Jesus in the other Gospels. While the latter do have phrases anticipating what is later emphatic in John, like: 'No man knows the Son but the Father neither knows any man the Father save the Son . . .' (Matt. 11.27), they do not translate that doctrine as to the 'status' of Jesus in the way John does into the exchanges of 'ordinary' ministry. John's Jesus speaks within transcendence. 'I came', he says, 'to save the world:' 'before Abraham came to be I am:' 'I and my Father are one'. Such words of Jesus according to John have led some readers to pose the suggestion: 'He was either mad or divine, either an imbecile or God', and those who put the issue that way find assurance in opting for divinity.

But such a formulation is totally astray, if not perverse. To think these the alternatives is to misconstrue what the Incarnation means. It is not about omniscience going around first pretending not to be such and then giving it free rein. It is not about a human annexing the divine so that we might truly say: 'That man – God!' Nor is it about God in some human surcease that abandons eternal Being. It is not about a masquerade to bewilder immediate disciples and mislead the centuries. What John hears Jesus saying he hears in the long aftermath of the experience of what he said and who he proved to be.

It is imperative for faith's decision to understand that
the formula: 'Jesus was/is God' says what is so, but in saying
it, does not avoid saying what is not so. It is comparable to
that other dubious phrase about Mary as 'the mother of
God' — clearly a blasphemous concept if we meant by it that
the being of God originates in the womb of Jesus' mother.
It is legitimate about her only in the sense that she was the
earthly instrument of his Incarnation, the 'handmaid' of 'the
Word made flesh.' Similarly, with 'Jesus is God.' It *could* be
taken to mean that the predicate 'God' is exhausted in the
subject 'Jesus,' as if one were to say: 'The play is Shakespeare,'
which would be true of *Hamlet* but untrue of the dramatist.
Only by adding '. . . the Son' to the statement 'Jesus is God . . .'
do we avoid the ambiguity — though it is sounder never to
have 'God' in a predicate. For God's is not the name of a
genus attaching to a variety of subjects, unless, that is, we
are pagans saying: 'Jupiter is God,' 'Caesar is God.' 'God was
in Christ' is the right, the Biblical, formula by which to
express the divineness of Jesus, veritable and real, not a
diversionary usurpation of all that we mean by the transcendent rulership and sovereignty of God, but expressing the
quality of these in the human idiom of the love that comes
and cares and suffers, which love — Jesus — is pre-eminently
'God manifest in flesh.' And it takes all that God is in order
to be so, just as the entire dramatist is necessary to, and
present in, the drama which fulfills him. All this we mean
by the relation of 'the Father and the Son.'

Returning to John from this important excursus into
theology we appreciate how false it is to set up the alternative
'mad or divine.' 'God was in Christ' in terms compatible with
authentic humanity. The being of God is not of a sort to
require us to identify His incarnate presence in terms of
deciding against insanity. That has to be said not only on
the grounds of theology, but on the evidence of Matthew,
Mark and Luke.

How, then, should we understand the language of the
Johannine Jesus which has incurred such unhappy
misconstruing? What shall we say of one who says; 'He that
eats my flesh dwells in me;' or: 'If any man thirst let him come
to me and drink,' or who speaks of himself impersonally and

says: This is life eternal that they should know Thee and Jesus Christ whom Thou hast sent'? While invitations like 'Come to me and I will give you rest' elswhere have something of this Johannine aura, and while John unfailingly returns to 'real' situations of blood and sweat, there is this distinctive character about his whole portraiture. Where is the clue?

Does it not lie, plainly, in the genius of interpretation in the long comprehension of prospective and gathering conviction? If we ask: 'Is he giving us the very words of Jesus?' the answer has to be Yes and No, asking as we do so what 'actual words' are. None of the Gospels are stenographic record or verbatim speech. All have come through the sift of memory and the mind of discipleship, and John's most of all. But that, unless we think of vocal syllables, does not disqualify them. We do not ask whether Hamlet ever said: 'The world is out of joint. O cursed spite . . .' We recognise the word as the truth of him. They speak the Prince himself.

But the reader protests: 'John was not a dramatist.' His Gospel, to be sure, is not theatre, but it is literature and he is creatively responsible for what he does with events, with chronology, with the drama of confrontation studied in chapter 2, and with the task of the faith at his own Ephesus. As just now quoted, he has Jesus talking impersonally, putting into words his whole mission, his disciples' Eucharist, his people's preservation, as these had come to be in the sequel to the story. If the sequel was truly his, then the words are also. It is not that John is ascribing to Jesus what had no warrant: it is that the warrant comes clear, and comes true, in what perspective tells.

The great prayer, for example, in John 17, before Jesus in 18.1 went out and crossed the Kedron, is very different from the scene in Gethsemane and the feel of the Synoptic Gospels. It reads almost like a final testament after a retrospect of decades. Its past tenses 'these have known . . .' and 'the world has hated them . . .' belong with a present (of the writer) which was then a future, but is now a 'future' that has possessed its meaning only in becoming past. John discerns what the meaning was and rightly credits it to Jesus.

It may help us to appreciate what John is doing by reference to other history. For merely to chronicle facts or

stay in a calendar is not to write history. Narrative has to
deepen into comprehension. Thucydides, for example,
among the Greeks found it essential to compose speeches
to embody the issues and to draw out from events the themes
of politics which were his consuming interest and the *raison
d'être* of history itself. The real nature of power and the
subtleties of politics could not be told in bare narrative bereft
of the thrust and feel of action. John's consuming interest
was not politics — shrewd as his perceptions were — but the
mystery of grace and the self-giving of God.

So, alert to confrontation as the marrow of the story about
Jesus and Jerusalem, he is ready to place the cleansing of
the Temple at the outset of the narrative, and to find the
disciples, or rather some of them, recruited to Jesus from
John the Baptist, not from lakeside fishing, not from laying
aside nets, but as initiates 'coming to see where Jesus dwelt'
as 'the lamb of God.' There is clearly hindsight here — and
creative writing. If the disciples had really known Jesus at
first, by that term, 'lamb of God,' with its overtones of
Messianic suffering and sacrifice, how could they have been
so uncomprehending, as the others Gospels have them —
and John too — in the course of Jesus' ministry? Either one
is wrong, or the other, if we stay with mere chronology. Both
are right, if we perceive a reading of the future as if it were
already present, as futures indeed are in many 'presents'. A
wedding day contains the future of a wedded life, perhaps
betrayal, tragedy or long consummation. Every ploughman
means a harvest and, assuming prospering elements, his
sowing has the reaping within it. John is describing and
presenting Jesus in the present of a latent future and
letting that future invite disciples in its ultimate terms.
Andrew and Philip certainly heard the call and followed 'the
lamb of God' in a knowledge that lay ahead of them but
which only came because they followed.

Occasions of this order are the very gist of John's authorship. He accompanies the Synoptics but from his own
perspective — a perspective which both needs and supposes
what they give. But the fusion of the four is not well
understood by some 'harmony' of them which purports to
insert incidents into a single sequence. For this is to suppose

that narrative for its own sake, rather than interpretation, is their sole concern. There are points of immediate dating where John has been seen to be more accurate than the others and he is always careful to have a timing. For he is not writing fantasy. Nevertheless, he shapes what he writes according to a pattern of 'signs' and 'I am's' and by a conscious selection of incidents within a scheme of presentation in which we have to listen for the clues.

Take the cryptic exchanges between Jesus and Nathaniel in 1.45-51. The latter is a doubtful hearer of the Messianic rumour but sincere in his Messianic hope — a detail we can recognise in the fact of Nathaniel being 'under the fig tree' when invited to Jesus. For 'every man under his vine and under his fig tree' was the scenario of Messiah's day. Nathaniel's otherwise obscure response, greeting Messiah-Jesus with discipleship, evokes Jesus' salute to a right sincerity contrasted with the guile of Jacob. Reference to Jacob opens into imagery of the final significance of Jesus drawn from Jacob's ladder. John has the first disciples discovering Jesus in the prospective terms of matured faith.

The familiar passage in 3.1-16, with Nicodemus visiting 'Jesus by night' is another case in point. Here it is hard to see where the immediate story ends and the evangelist takes over in discourse. This 'master of the people' as his name implies — and as so addressed by Jesus — to a degree accepts, or at least pays tribute to, Jesus' teaching but proves unfamiliar with 'birth from above' and the 'wind of the Spirit.' Do we not have here an epitome of all we have in Matthew, Mark and Luke, concerning what transpired between Jesus teaching and a constituency both conceding he had an authority and yet elusive about obeying it? Then the passage moves into a full statement of the ultimate faith prospectively articulate where it had earlier begun. How 'God so loved the world that He gave His only-begotten Son' has more the ring of apostolic preaching and of credal faith than of the beginnings in Galilee. Yet there is no falsification, since the one derives from the other.

A similar conclusion compels itself upon us when we study the long discourse in John 6 about 'the bread of life.' It arises out of the feeding of the multitude, which all four Gospels

tell. But 'eating ... and living by me' in no way fits the
immediacies of that desert occasion as Jesus let the crowds
disperse. Does it not rather pre-suppose the theme of the
Eucharist in the early Church, understood as the sacramental participation of faith in the 'mystery' of the death
of Christ? 'The bread of life' is the common thread that joins
the story and the rite. There was no sharp controversy and
no reference to a 'heavenly manna' when the people sat in
orderly fashion and the disciples moved among them with
the baskets. These transpired in John's own context at the
time he wrote. In that setting 'the bread and the partaking,'
from the original scene, (when there was no mention of 'the
blood and the drinking') took on and took over the
bearings of the later day. John's 'history,' here as everywhere,
is what history came to mean. As literature, his Gospel came
into being — he would claim — by the impulse of that
meaning and by the realisation that a history was what it had
to tell. For John did not write a treatise, nor a diary, nor an
essay: he wrote a Gospel.

Perhaps the most striking example of the overlap, involved in his writing, between the story he tells and the scene
where he lives is the episode of the blind man who, after
being given sight by Jesus, was 'cast out of the synagogue.'
In John's context there was a territory of sharp contention
between Christian and Jew, a territory in which those
suspected of being pseudo or crypto by either party were
the core of dispute. Jews who might have a mind for Messiah-
Jesus but hesitated about the Eucharist and 'Gentiles un-
circumcised' or Christians less than whole-hearted about
these, were tugged either way by rival demands of 'no
compromise.' Or they were suspect as possibly spies from
the other side whose doubtful loyalty would be dangerous.
The hesitant are always so regarded where issues of great
import and high emotion are at stake. It is not that the
Johannine community is 'anti-semitic' here. 'The Jews,' as a
'label' in this context refers to adversarial people, from John's
angle, who were either hostile or dubious, not to a whole
race or culture. Indeed the one term is used in the Gospel
both for the whole identity and for the particular entity
within it, and it is used, of course, by one who was himself

a Jew. Precise allegiance, belonging that was not covert, became sharply urgent when Christianity ceased to be a *religio licita* in Roman eyes. A faith that might need dying for could not be a theme of ambiguity.

The episode in John 9 bears all the marks of this situation. The parents of the man, when questioned, wish to avoid responsibility. 'He is of age, ask him,' they say. The interview between the man and the establishment carries the overtones of Ephesus and finally he is cast out, to be found and solaced by Jesus himself in gentle confirmation of embryonic faith. What starts in ignorant gratitude ends in articulate belief — which was precisely the shape of Christian adherence as John's community knew it and enlarged it in the stress of their own time.

But if that context imbues the telling what, it will be asked, of the actual event in — was it? — Jericho? Other Gospels bear ample witness to the fact that such healings occurred. There was, for example, the blind Bartimaeus. In such as he there is the gist of the story. What John's telling instills into it has a kinship with the truth perceived in Saul's conversion, namely that what new Christians suffer for faith's sake is one with the suffering of Jesus, seeing that the enmity implied is akin to the rejection leading to the Cross. That sense of solidarity between the Christian and the Christ could hardly have been known at once to Bartimaeus. It only emerged to later perspective. But it was a precious reality in Ephesus and one properly deduced from the original event. The other point arising in John's version is that pride of 'establishment' can entail a blindness to positive good. The blind man, after all, had become now a sighted person. Yet the rejoicing, the celebration, proper to such a liberation, was — literally — lost to sight by the self-concern of a religious institution. John brings out subtly the significance of that other 'blindness.' It remains a lesson Christian institutions themselves have since needed, when privilege, or pride, or orthodoxy, or tradition, have resisted the disconcerting evidence of the Holy Spirit. How deftly the whole story pits the simple confession of experience against the prejudice of place and power. 'One thing I know,' in my ignorance of your niceties, 'now I see.'

Examples could be multiplied in John of this skilful inter-
penetration of times and meanings. We come to realise
that there is a second meaning to the familiar phrase, so
prominent throughout the New Testament, namely 'according to the Scriptures.' It can mean not only the precedents
present or cited from sacred Hebrew writings, to which, as
we have seen, the pattern of Jesus is believed to conform.
It can also be adapted to cover the New Testament itself, both
Gospels and Epistles. It is 'according to them' that we have
Jesus as Christianity knows him. 'The Word' is according to
'the flesh,' in the sense that the whole garnered import of
Jesus is apprehended communally *from* a history by a
corpus of experience through pens that set it down as
Scripture. Later, in a process we do not here explore, comes
the community's canonisation of those writings (and
rejection of others) not, thereby, to endow them with
authority but appropriately to recognise the authority they
are deemed to possess within themselves. That process
through three centuries serves to symbolise the necessary
inter-play between history as event and history-telling as
perception. The corporate perception, enshrined in Scripture, becomes in its turn also an event. This does not mean
that the *kerugma*, the thing heralding, is all there is of the
thing heralded. Quite the contrary. But it does mean that
the preaching as a content and the preaching as an activity
belong inseparably together, the Christ *via* the
Christians constituting Christianity.

The emergence of 'new' Scriptures themselves, the instinct
to treat them as such (whereas they had originally been *ad
hoc* letters, local circulars, or writings on the way to status)
and to set them alongside the traditional 'old' writings for
purposes of lection and tuition, all tally with this telling of
the Christ and the Christ in the telling which we have been
at pains to comprehend.

Nowhere is the interplay more pointed than in the great
commission at the end of Matthew. It has a very Johannine
flavour, in that it participates in later perspective. The
baptismal formula, 'in the Name of the Father, and of the
Son, and of the Holy Spirit,' surely belongs with a later day
than those first disciples. Yet the terms of the sending, the

assurance of the warrant, the pledge of the unfailing presence — all these belonged with that first time and place because they were the truth of its future.

In sum, then, the four Gospels in the manner of their genesis and the shape of their consensus are the documents of a decision — a decision of which Jesus was the theme and the Christian society was the issue. They are at once both product and result, as the scriptuarising of the Christ, written for an immediate context but destined — as the sequel was to prove — to perpetuate the data of that decision, in hallowed form, for the centuries to come and so to constitute a literary testament of faith. The processes of which they were the climax occupy the time-gap between the beginning of their story and their finalising of its record. Christian scholarship has engaged that interlude in long and careful interrogation. The Epistles, of course, fall within it, with the Book of the Acts of Apostles tracing the westward direction of expansion. Those other documents of the New Testament are the light it throws on the setting out of which its Gospels achieved their memorialising of Jesus. Fragmentary those other documents may be, leaving many points in tantalising silence. But they suffice to convey the dynamism, the *élan*, and the quality of heart with which the Gospel told by evangelists in the Gospels was told by evangelism in the world. Either telling explains and undergirds the other. Together they charted, and chartered, Christianity.

CHAPTER 4

The Christ-dwelling Life

> 'O teach these wounds to bleed
> In me: me, so to read
> This book of loves, thus writ
> In lines of death, my life may copy it
> With loyal cares.
> O let me here claim shares:
> Yield something in Thy sad prerogative...'

Richard Crashaw of the 17th century may seem to some an extravagant poet. But these lines of his, in their sharp imagery, do capture the character of New Testament aspiration to live within the significance of the Cross of Jesus. The Gospels, as we have seen, concentrate steadily on the passion story. They are 'books of love writ in lines of death.' The Epistles, in turn, 'with loyal cares' in personal and communal affairs 'teach' the churches in the copying of the lines they read in Jesus. It is this theme of 'the imitation of Christ' — understanding the meaning wisely — which takes us to the heart of Christian ethics and underlies the meaning of Christian baptism. There was for the early church an unlearning of the ways of selfish man only in the learning of the way of Christ.

Both ensued in the setting of pagan society across the wide dispersion of communities from Anatolia to Spain, from Rome to Carthage. The excesses of that society were familiar enough to philosophers who deplored them or Stoic purists who despaired of them. The great Aristotle had long before confined the possibility of 'the good life' to the well-born and well endowed. No 'kingdom open to all' made sense in his book. The socially disadvantaged must necessarily be for ever at the base of the human pyramid, its moral apex inaccessible to those once born in deprivation and ignorance. And was it not a constant feature of Jewish anxiety about such risky hopeful notions as Gentle inclusion that they jeopardised the whole ethos of 'the chosen people'? How could the moral law survive unless the ceremonial law remained inviolate? Pearls should not be gaily cast before swine, a practice in which, as Jewry saw it, Paul was dubiously engaged.

Our first duty, then, in studying the resembling of Jesus in the vocation of his churches is to appreciate the reality of that dispersal which the New Testament serves. The Epistles witness to an apostolic solicitude for common standards and mutual relation. There is a nascent authority taking stock, and taking care, about a whole. But it is scattered in the here and there of the Mediterranean scene. It lives in its localisms, whether impoverished villages in Galatia, maritime centres like Corinth, or cities with their ampitheatres and academies like Ephesus and Colosse. It lives too 'in Caesar's household.' Its people, like the inscription over the Cross, have names Hebrew, Greek and Latin.

For all these localities there is, according to Paul, another location, that 'in Christ.' All humanity, to be sure, is 'in Adam,' in the sense of sharing creaturehood and mortality. But within this human family is a new society of faith in Jesus, a society for which there are no pre-requisites of birth, or culture, or refinement, or locale. The vital particular is that of discipleship. It is a discipleship which constitutes a localising of fellowship where-ever it obtains. It is this 'anywhere-in-faith' which Paul denotes by his territorial name: 'in Christ.' Where there is 'gathering in his (Christ's) name,' there is holy ground.

It is important to appreciate this feature of the New Testament's scattered unity both in relation to, and in contrast from, the ancient significance of Jerusalem. That city in the earlier idiom of so many of the new Christians was 'the holy place,' the city of the Temple where authentic worship had its singular locale. It is true that already Jewish communities were one 'in Torah' far away from their holy city. This synagogue movement intensified urgently after the Fall of Jerusalem. Yet the mystique of Jerusalem endured. For it was — in that haunting phrase of the prophets — 'the place of the Name.' So Solomon had prayed in the inaugural prayer at the Temple's first dedication: '. . . that Thine eyes may be open towards this house night and day, toward the

place of which Thou hast said: 'My Name shall be there.' '
'The place and the Name' became inseparable. The grim Yad
va Sham Memorial to the victims of the Holocaust recalls
it with anguish in Israeli Jerusalem today. 'The Name of the
Lord at Jerusalem' was no mere label. The place was the
rendezvous where promise had fulfilment, where David
accomplished in a central stronghold what Moses had
dreamed and Joshua, who never knew the city, had begun.
In the possession of 'the holy land,' thus consummated in the
symbol of the city, its people possessed themselves of a
covenanted Lord. They read the pledge of their security, their
peace and benediction. They revered the Name in the
sanctity of the place and knew it as the focus of their prayers,
the home of their festivals, the sanctuary of their ritual. It
was there that Hebrews ought to worship.

The Christian heirs of this tradition broke it open in a
territorial emancipation from the necessity of locale.
'Beginning at Jerusalem' their habitation might reach to 'the
uttermost parts of the earth.' Their faith in 'the Word made
flesh' meant that Jesus had become for them 'the place of
the Name,' the truth-in-personality where God was known
and where, therefore, He might be universally addressed. The
'ground' of Jesus could be everywhere. For it was there, where-
ever two or three were met around it. Every place was thereby
holy city, holy land. In their writings they spoke of 'the
temple of his body' and themselves its 'living stones.' Nor,
in doing so, did the Jews among them think themselves
disloyal. Location in Jesus was, for them, the logic of the
precedent place and the eternal Name. Jerusalem was not
dispossessed, it was justified in becoming, as Paul had it, 'the
mother of us all.'

It is in this sense that dispersal in the New Testament is
to be described as 'Christ-dwelling life.' Territory might still
be sentimentally loved for associations' sake. But, in the literal
sense of the Greek word they lived in *par oikia*, sojourning
anywhere. From this 'footlooseness,' if we may so speak, there
followed a deeper meaning still. If God was revealed and
pledged in Jesus and in the terms of his Cross, and if they
dwelt in that significance loyally, then they, in their living,
became — by inference — themselves 'the place of the Name.'

'Christ in you' is the familiar phrase in the Epistles: each of the faithful in their sphere and relationship being an expression of Christ. 'I in them . . . that the world may know' is how the fourth evangelist phrases the will of Jesus in his communion with the Father. 'I am glorified in them,' he says, making his disciples the living testament of his whole significance.

This is the source and sanction of 'the imitation of Christ,' of the Christ-dwelling life in the double sense of disciples being where he is identified for who he is, and they being who and how they are because of him. But before taking its measure it is well to dispose of a misconception which has arisen in many quarters, scholarly and popular, through a sad misreading of the passage in 2 Cor. 5.16 with which we began in chapter 1. Paul writes there about 'not knowing Christ after the flesh.' Some have alleged that he meant a disinterest in the actual Jesus, a total unconcern with what had transpired in Galilee. An odd conclusion in itself, it is allied with the notion, or the charge, that Paul was in fact responsible for turning the simple message of Jesus into the subtle abstraction of a cosmic Christ. Paul was, according to this, the real architect of traditional Christology and, as such, a perverter of what should have been the gospel according to Jesus.

Some aspects of what is at stake here will concern us in chapter 6. The immediate issue is his meaning in the quoted passage. He does not write about knowing or not knowing *Jesus* but Christ. His theme, in the context of the integrity of ministry (his earlier topic), is that self-seeking is repudiated in true service. Motivation is not by the calculating, devious criteria of immoral man, nor by the cynical assessments to which these are liable. 'We do not think of people that way,' he says. 'Such attitudes no longer hold for us'. It is not acquaintance with anyone that he is writing about but distrustful, dismissive suspicions about each and all. Most of all he does not think of *the* Christ that way. He does not see that role characterised by selfish nationalistic pride or turning on exclusive factors, a Messiahship that participates in the evils it should redeem. Worldly standards have ceased to count in the way he identifies Messiah. For the very theme of Messianic hope has been transformed in the Messiah Jesus has been. Far from being a disclaimer about Jesus the passage hinges on the very decision we have been studying and marks Paul as truly sharing it.

That we need not stay to suppose Paul disengaged from Jesus is amply corroborated not only by a right reading of what he writes to Corinth here, but by the clear evidence of all his letters. To be sure they leave the telling of the Jesus story to the Gospels which, in embyro, were already under-taking it as he wrote. But his letters breathe the example of Jesus at every turn. They echo the very text of his discourses and draw their sense and urgency from him.

To be sure, direct verbatim quotation is not frequent, nor would it be the proper test. The Gospels themselves are literary constructs presenting what was remembered from the preaching of Jesus in the form the evangelists set for it, as we have earlier seen. His sayings had become part of the mental furniture of the communities. For Jesus himself had never written his own texts, nor left documents from his own hand. His reliance had been entirely on the receptive discipleship his message kindled. It was in that sense John has him say: 'I have given them Thy word.' Paul certainly shared in this mind-shaping from the lips of his Lord, as did all his co-authors within the Christian Scripture.

According to Luke, he concludes his moving farewell to the elders from Ephesus with the call to 'remember the words of the Lord Jesus, how he said: 'It it is more blessed to give than to receive' ' — a saying that eluded all the four evangelists in their own writing. Elsewhere such remember-ing dominates his theology. 'Bless those who persecute you,' Paul tells the Romans. (12.14). Where did he learn so if not from Luke 6.28? 'Be at peace among yourselves,' he urges the Thessalonians (1.5.13) in tune with Mark 9.50. 'Rejoice evermore,' in the same letter (1.5.16) was exactly Jesus' bidding in blessing the disciples (Luke 6.23). On the Colossians (3.13) he presses the duty of forgiveness in the very words of eg. Matt. 6.14. Again he tells the Romans how he is 'persuaded by the Lord Jesus that there is nothing unclean of itself' but only as it is deemed so by the user. His very Greek here is uncannily close to the passage in Mark

7.15 where Jesus had said the same. In the same passage he appeals to brother not to judge brother nor put a stumbling-block in his way. There is no mistaking where he found such counsel. He writes about 'the meekness and gentleness of Christ' as if his hearers would know the phrase as familiar already with the currency Matthew was to immortalise in 11.28-30.

Reminiscences inspire him to allusions which, though not verbatim, are clear enough. He knows how 'to be abased' and how 'uplifting' (for others) can follow from it. He counsels his correspondents to be content among, and with, 'the lowly.' When he speaks of the transformation of life in 2 Cor. 3 he recalls the narrative of the Transfiguration. He goes so far as to summon his readers to an imitation of himself but only on the ground of his own imitation of Jesus, and always with the confidence that those who respond will, like a glad contagion, be themselves a spur to imitation by others again. Thus in the daily life of the churches the pattern and likeness of Jesus will be steadily reproduced and perpetuated.

Nor are we involved here only in verbal echoes and narrative recollection, indicating how the moral education through the Epistles is in step with the history-telling in the nascent Gospels. Paul's thought goes further. Jesus has come to constitute for him a personal Torah, the embodiment of the ancient law as the new law of love made concrete in biography. At the heart of that conviction is the fact of Jesus' obedience to the Father's will — an obedience of which the Cross is the measure and the climax. Such love is 'the fulfilling of the law,' and so 'the end of the law' in the sense that, thereby, law has seen its consummation. It follows that all sense of Christian obligation has to be referred back to this criterion.

Paul is by no means alone in this perception of what it is to be 'in Christ.' He is part of a wide consensus. We have been occupied with him as our first mentor only because of the ill-judged notion — as it must be seen to be — that he ignored or disesteemed the actual Jesus. The rest of New Testament writers, in their own idiom, stand in the same tradition. The Johannine Epistles breathe the life of a love given and received and, therefore, controlling all relationships. 'Commandment,' as in Romans, is fulfilled in the 'love of brethren.' All are addressed as 'children' because the divine love has inaugurated and consecrated a single 'family.' The Letters are written not to teach but to celebrate what the readers already know, namely that 'love is of God,' verified in the self-giving of 'the sent one' who is the reality 'in the flesh' of the divine love that God is. 'We love because He first loved us.' The love that can, and must, be imperative in human life is only so in having been, and for ever remaining, affirmative in God.

This confidence, demanding this summons, means 'walking as he walked.' (1.2.6.) Continuing therein means 'abiding in what you have heard from the beginning.' (1.2.24). Disciples are 'in the world, as he was,' not only in the sense of what they undergo but in how they undergo it. (2 John 6). The test of conduct within and from the community of faith is not some rubric of form but the inward logic of the Christ-character, not precepts except as also indwelling. The writer called John, in his own quality of soul and pen, reads and speaks the same language as Paul.

The First Epistle of Peter — again with a distinctive personal tone — reinforces and shares the same perspective. 'As he is so are we in this world' of John's logic recurs precisely in Peter with the stress on 'holiness' (1.15) and lowliness of mind (3.8-9). Association goes back further here, in contrast to John, into precedents from psalm and prophet. But these are subsumed into the inclusive pattern of Jesus himself and the fact of his readiness to suffer. The Lord has left an example, a *hupogrammos* (2.21), 'a copy such as writing masters set before their pupils for their reproduction,' the calligraphy of patience and gentleness. Like Paul in 1 Cor. 4.11, Peter (in 2.20) uses the word *kolaphizo*, (to buffet) recalling, we may guess, the very narrative of the passion of Jesus, where Mark has the word (14.65). But the associations are more than strikingly verbal: they are emphatically visual. Two passages in 1 Peter have a strong note of the eye-witness at the crucifixion. 'When he was reviled he did not revile . . .' and 'in his own self he bore our sins as far as the tree.' (2.23 and 24). But such vividness of recollection is always on behalf of the impulse to a like vocation. Nowhere is the interweaving of the life of Jesus and the calling of the church more vivid than in 1 Peter, while 'the suffering servant' of Isaiah 42 and 53 is never out of mind.

The Letter to the Hebrews, however we resolve the question of its authorship, is similarly immersed in the actuality of Jesus as the Christ. It has its own singular philosophy, its themes of worship, law, covenant and priesthood, and its own subtle nuances and allusions. But all are set within the context of the teaching, serving, suffering Christ. The analogies of Moses, and Israel, Sinai and wilderness trials, entry into Canaan, the rites of the Temple, are all recruited to teach and interpret the imitable significance of Jesus. Such imitation is both mystical and practical. Liturgically patterned, it issues in 'good conduct', (2.12) clear conscience (3.16), warm hospitality (13.1), and timely compassion (13.16). The call throughout is: 'consider him ...' (3.1 and 12.3), making Jesus the 'analogy' to be invoked in all things, the theme of our contemplation. When the Epistle to the Hebrews reaches its final benediction the strong preamble concerns all that God did through 'our Lord Jesus', as the ground of our being 'made perfect in every good work to do His will' by the energy within us (lit. the 'doing') 'well-pleasing in His sight', and all — 'through Jesus Christ'. Such is the eloquent harmony within the New Testament of the Jesus in the story and the Christ in the heart and community.

But to review in this way the grounding of the self-education of the churches through the Epistles within the narrative frame of the Gospels does not complete the picture of New Testament integration of the one with the other. It is not only in the rehearsal, or the echoing, of what Jesus taught, or the pattern of character he exemplified, which availed for Christian identity. There was a deeper dimension still captured in the poem's line with which we began: 'Let these wounds bleed in me'. It was the suffering of Jesus, in fulfilling Messiahship, which was to become, not exemplary only, but also a principle by which selfhood in each and all is to be received and fulfilled. This takes us into the significance of the passion of Christ and the baptism of the Christian. The Christ-dwelling life, we might almost say, is the Christ-formed death into life.

Here, in a way which will clarify as we proceed, the Christian faith, so to say, stumbled upon a mystery which had long engrossed the Buddist mind of Asia and, at the very time when Christianity was coming to be, was working profound changes within Buddhism itself from the Theravada (Hinayana) tradition to the Mahayana. There is nowhere, between disparate faiths, a more fascinating situation of divergence with concurrence than here, between the Buddha of the Sangha and the Christ of the churches. But let us hold it in the margin while we explore the Cross and baptism equation. What do Paul, and others, mean when they speak of 'being crucified with Christ.'?

There has been a tendency in some quarters to dismiss the matter as a 'Christ-mysticism,' exotic, elusive and probably meaningless outside a coterie of devotion. We need a longer patience. 'Mysticism' anyway is a loaded term. If we use it for what Paul meant by 'dying with Christ' we must appreciate how practical, how down-to-earth, how energising, was its relevance. It has been well observed how his catalogue of afflictions in 2 Cor. 4.8-11 follows very closely the vocabulary of the passion story of Jesus. There is a rhythm in the paradoxes of the passage — affliction, perplexity, desolation, and crushing adversity, countered by 'not crushed, not despairing, not forsaken, not destroyed.' It tallies closely with the same sequences in the events around Gethsemane. Paul identifies it all as 'carrying in the body the death of Jesus that the life of Jesus may be manifested.' Paul is not writing about fantasy or even contemplation: he is describing a life of action. But he calls it dying with Jesus and 'newness of life.'

What, then, did he mean? The answer returns us to the crucial passage in 2. Cor. 5 where he reads in the death of Jesus the death of all. 'If one man died for all then all died in him.' There is an initial meaning that to kill what is man is to kill all mankind. Cain's murder of Abel is inclusive fratricide: for that is the logic of the enmity. The Qur'ān makes this point in Surah 5.32: 'If anyone slays a human being, unless it be for a soul slain (i.e. the *lex talionis*) or for corrupting the earth, it will be as though he had slain all

mankind.' Any such *lex talionis* is altogether excluded in the
Gospel, but the main principle is constant, namely that the
many are present in the one. For 'any man's death diminishes
mankind.'

Paul's meaning, however, goes deeper by far. When he
writes that: 'Christ died *for* our sins,' at least his first
meaning of that elusive preposition *for* is that it was our sins
that occasioned his death. This unanimous conviction of the
New Testament about the Cross as happening through 'the
sin of the world' was central to our study in chapter 1. The
point now is that it constitutes the Cross of Jesus as symbol,
within history, of that about human-ness in us all which, by
alert decision, we must acknowledge in penitence in order
to renounce in life. What crucifies Jesus may be seen by some
as merely routine, ordinary, even miniscule as a particular
in the wide and awful perspective of the past and present.
Have there not been vaster, sharper, more horrendous
tragedies and crimes? Certainly so, in terms of quantity and
range. Crucifixions, after all, in Roman days, and their
counterparts since, have been legion times legion. But in its
quality the will to the judicial murder of Jesus has, for
Christian perception, the claim to count as representatively human and representatively wrong, a deed which in
its motives and its meaning incriminates us all, a deed from
which there is no private exoneration.

It stands, then, in our eyes as the veritable symptom of our
perversity, of the evil potential of the selves we are. 'Were
you there when they crucified my Lord?' — haunting and
authentic as song and a lament — is a question we must, and
yet need not, ask. For to know our own selves is to know our
complicity. The Cross identifies the history which implicates
us all. As such it is a powerful negation of the selves we are,
a negation to which we are required to consent. It stands,
in its evil contours as the human deed, for that which we
must repudiate within ourselves.

But the self it constrains us to negate, to let die, is not the
only self we ever can be. Quite the contrary: it is the self astray
from its true being. The Buddha learned and taught that
there is a self we must renounce. But for many of his
communities and disciples that self is all the self there ever

was or can be, a selfish self set in the illusion of personality.
Escape lay in *ab*negation, in the discipline which 'saw through'
the illusion and so disarmed the self in disenchantment with
time and ambition and possessions. That 'unselfing' was
based on a scepticism about the significance of history and
the relevance of a future. It turned on a persuasion about
transitoriness as the sole consideration in evaluating
existence — a consideration which, all things being fleeting,
disqualified all positive acceptance of life's challenge, except
the one not to allow it to deceive us.

Yet, if we insist on the radical difference, how close in one
way to the logic of the Cross the Buddha was. There *is* a self
to deny, to let-not-be, or, in Paul's word, to 'mortify.' There
is a saying No! awaited from the would-be Christian, a No!
to that in them which Jesus' Cross exposes and indicts. It
is in this sense Paul says we have to count his death for ours,
to be crucified with Christ. As victimisers of this 'victim' we
humans have to die with him and in him in that capacity
of ours which had him crucified. The rigorous discipline
of the Eightfold Path of Buddhism perceives how devious
we can be in our corruptibility, our mindedness towards what
the Biblical psalmist called 'presumptuous sins.' Hence the
watchfulness and self scrutiny that Path enjoined upon
disciples in attaining right thinking, right renouncing, right
concentration, and the rest. In the New Testament it is as
if all these requisites are dramatised, drawn into recognition
of their task by the measure of what, for lack of them, men
did to Jesus. They are then no longer themes of theory and
analysis, and so of 'skilled insight' as Buddhist Scriptures
phrased it, but responses to the meaning of an event.

The first Christians saw that event as also liberation. It may
be that the very effort, by scrutiny and abnegation, to
discipline ourselves into 'rightness' (by whatever religion
identified), only perpetuates our self-centredness. The quest
for freedom from pride becomes occasion of it. The self
persists within our very disciplines either as congratulation
or as a sharper self-pre-occupation. Our own shadow accompanies our effort to detach from it. Perhaps it is here that
'the love of Christ' has its further role. For, though it leaves
to us the decision of response, it leaves us no ground for

self-congratulation, since it is all of debt. The No! to self becomes Yes! to Christ, a Yes which restores us to ourselves but in the new capacity of debt to grace. The negation is then a way into 'newness of life,' not an abnegation of the adventure of selfhood and the encounters of the world, the senses, the society, of our mortal span.

It was in these terms that the New Testament church understood and accepted baptism by the analogy of death. We find it most explicitly in the Fourth Gospel and in the Epistles of Paul, notably that to the Romans. The Cross became for faith the symbol of a 'death to sin' and the resurrection of 'life in righteousness.' The sense of an ending in physical death is the most radical interrogation of what our life is and means. Nothing so concentrates the mind as to life's significance. The fact of our present reprieve from an undoubted demise makes us take total stock of who and why we are. What better analogy, then, for the will to an inclusive decision about the self which is alive — a decision reached by reference to the Cross of Jesus? Baptism both symbolised and transacted that decision. It expressed a forsaking and a becoming, an emigration and an immigration, a being dead and yet alive anew. The death and resurrection of Jesus became the logic and the point of their moral counterpart within the personal disciples. They were to 'reckon' the old self to be dead and so, as it were, disinherited of claim and place, whereby the new self could come to be.

To Jewish Christians the long analogy of the Exodus and Passover was precious here. In that memorialised event they celebrated the ending of bondage and the possession of freedom. They were out of the one and into the other. Through waters — the Red Sea and the Jordan — they understood themselves transformed by passage. With the further imagery of washing, Christian baptism took over these graphic associations and spoke of 'Christ our Passover . . .' They identified themselves by the experience of a past they had abandoned and a present they had found. The past was the self mirrored in what reared the Cross. The present was a selfhood 'risen with Christ.'

That past-present situation was not, to use terms of gram-

mar, the 'simple' tense but the 'continuous.' The old Israelites
reverted often to their Egypt in cowardice or sloth. But that
did not alter their liberation — a liberation to be con-
stantly taken up because once for all achieved. Of the same
order was Paul's 'reckon yourselves dead' to the claims of
sinful self — not a static, passive fact but a fact to be steadily
'realised' in will and deed.

Hence the role of that other great primary Christian
sacrament — Holy Communion. For the Eucharist
memorialised the death and resurrection of Jesus both as
history and as analogy. The bread and wine, broken and
poured, were, by Jesus' institution, the point of recalling
into the significance of his dying. They kept always in the
focus of worship 'the price of sin' and therein the truth about
ourselves. But they did so only in telling also how 'grace
abounded' in that very context. Thus they laid upon the
worshipper the steady claim to a self-awareness at once both
renouncing what it told about the self while receiving what
it enabled in the self's remaking in its image. 'It is the mystery
of yourselves which is laid upon the holy table,' Augustine
of Hippo told his readers, 'it is the mystery of yourselves that
you receive.'

Informed by the rite that inaugurated and shaped by the
rite that perpetuated their decision, the first Christians knew
themselves called to practise, in their own relationships, the
forgiveness they had received. The Cross, through baptism
and eucharist, bound them over to the work of love in the
world. They were to be associates of Christ's passion,
dwelling in its perspectives, its perception of the world. These
were at once utterly realist. How could they be otherwise in
such a light? But they were also imbued with hope and
anticipation. For the virtue in his Cross, through their
imitation of its patterns, promised the same potential in
others as they had known in themselves. Or, in the idiom
of John, the vine had its branches where its fruit was
borne. So 'let this mind be in you which was also in Christ
Jesus' because a sort of watchword in society, an enabling
principle of conduct, the condition of the Christ-dwelling life.

So it was that the apostles, as mentors of the new
communities, sought to overcome in these the patterns of

social and personal evil rife in Gentile, pagan living, and by the same token, to demonstrate to Jewish purists, sceptical of all 'breeds outside the law', that laxity and moral compromise were no part of the Gospel. Where-ever the New Testament Epistles enjoin and expound the ethical behaviour demanded by the new faith it is in the immediate context of the mental review of what that faith is. Likewise there are few doctrinal expositions which lack — in their very context — the express relation they bear to character and personal living. The Epistle to the Romans is a salient example. Given that chapters 9 to 11 are an obvious unity within themselves, chapter 12 begins with its inclusive: 'I beseech you, therefore . . .' in sequence to the foregoing chapters 1 to 8 which form a comprehensive treatise of Paul's doctrine. His appeal is grounded in his whole theology. Comparably the chapters of 1 Peter habitually move from faith to living, from the theme of the Christ to the temper of the Christian. 'If any one suffer as a Christian', it runs (in the only context outside the Book of Acts where the Greek text has *Christianos*) each is 'to glorify God in this name', that is, acknowledging the name worthily of its origin in 'the glory' that is Christ's.

There is an intriguing echo of the same vocation in the brief third letter of John, where the topic is hospitality. Early Christians, it is clear, were much travelled. In strange cities they sought out their fellows. Hence the need for commendation, both to accredit people on the move and protect communities from spies and infiltrators with malicious intent. Hence in turn the need for leadership and trusted personnel both to furnish and receive the commendations. The point of hospitality, says the Letter (v.6), is to facilitate all such transit 'worthily of God.' It would seem that the development of the role of 'elders' and 'bishops' belongs to this 'harmonising' of the approach to living with the appeal of the thing believed, both tuned to 'the glory of God.' The first Epistle of John has this mutuality of faith-conviction and life-quality as its central theme, making the divine love the great original and the human love the responsive action.

It is well to recall in this connection that when the Fourth Gospel gathers its Prologue around 'the Word made flesh . . . dwelling among us' it has in mind the divine disclosure, what grammarians would call the 'indicative.' But 'the Word' in the Hebraic tradition was also the 'imperative.' 'By the word of the Lord were the heavens made,' wrote the psalmist. The will of the Lord was executed, fulfilled, when the command via 'the word' was uttered. 'He commanded and they were created.' All that the Johannine tradition of 'the Word' means, namely the truth-through-personality of the Incarnation and the associations of divine wisdom implicit in the Logos, can be held to incorporate the commanding word also. The summons to our 'flesh' and sentient life belongs with 'the flesh' taken in divine self-giving. Thus the Incarnation becomes a truth about our humanity in being the truth about God. What is given to faith is required of the will. To discern in 'the Word' the divine nature is to discover the divine will for our own.

This 'imperative' implicit in the faith about Jesus is appropriately at the heart of contemporary 'liberation theology' notably in Latin America. 'Truth and imperative,' these theologians insist, 'are identical.' In the urgency of their passion for social righteousness against the injustice of structures there has to be an equal urgency to let the passion of Christ resolve all that, conceptually, we hold about God. Only then will our moral activisms have the right sort of anger, only then will our 'intellectual love of God,' which liberationists sometimes discount, be alerted to duty as well as to wonder. For there have been theologies which only indulge our ingenuity or bemuse our speculation.

That the Christ-dwelling life in the New Testament was squarely set for active righteousness and righteous action is plain in every epistle. But, when aligned with today's liberationists, does it not seem strangely modest and private, acquiescent about the wider world and, except in the vital issue of worship, posing no challenge to Caesar? 'Study to be quiet,' the Thessalonians are told, 'working with their hands to be able to give to the needy.' It is an ethic of gentle marriage and dutiful children, of peaceable living and honest citizenship. It pictures the watching world capable of good impressions that persuade to faith, not a world to be challenged in protest and defiance. The virtues of com-passion, affection, fervour and generosity within the

Christian communities are clear and lively enough. But do they otherwise affect the public scene or address the iniquities in public place and power? Do they undertake the sins of structures and the wrongs of class and market and forum? Was the theology of grace and the vocation to patient kindliness all that an epistle to Romans should contain? If we are studying Christian 'decision' how decisive was it?

It was decisive where it most needed to be, namely in its reading of the sovereignty of God by the credentials of Christ and its realism about the human situation. The first Christians lived by these with a nearer horizon of time than moderns see. The expectation of the 'appearing of Jesus,' the *parousia,* gave an immediacy to their sense of the future but did so with a dimension well able to endure beyond the misreading of chronology only later known to be implicit in that expectation. Their ethic was not based on any measure of brevity but on measures of eternity. Nevertheless, it was not for them to proceed on the wider stage of events and opportunity which would later become the setting of their long successors — and did so become only because of the legacy of that first obedience. They were a minority, a *religio illicita,* dwelling in catacombs and struggling, for their very survival by the very terms of their origin. Not for them the *magisterium,* the *ecclesia regnans,* of the hidden future.

Yet when that future transpired with its sharpened temptations and liabilities, the test of its responsibilities, the reproach of its waywardness, and the criterion of its obedience had been defined once and for all in the first and founding decision of faith. The name *Christianoi* did not denote a cave community, nor a school of thought. It described an allegiance compelled by Christ to live both realistically and redemptively within the wrongness of the world. Allegiance to such living under his authority held the clue by which to read and to meet the human situation whatever the exigencies of other times and places. If the centuries have changed almost out of recognition from the time and place of Thessalonians, Galatians and the Galileans first of all, what abides and avails is the significance for our minds and our wills of the Messiahship of Jesus, achieved and acknowledged.

It must start for us now in penitence, in a recognition of
sin private and structural, a will to apologise to God for all
that is perverse and malevolent in the way we are, in the
trivialising, brutalising distortions we commit against the
sanctity of nature, the benediction of sex, the trust of
techniques. It means a perception of the sacramental in all
the transactions and exchanges of the economic order and
the vicissitudes of the political arena. Faith in the Incarnation leaves no room for exoneration, but kindles, paradoxically, a heightened awareness of evil. Yet it is not an
awareness that despairs in aloofness or cynicism, but rather
has a mind to honesty and retrieval. This quality of the
founding faith in God through Christ, in a context far in
time and contrast from that of its initiation, can sustain the
dynamism necessary to answer the injustice, the oppression,
the desolation and the anguish which are today's counterpart of the Cross that Jesus knew. In the world as honesty
must own it to be, it is well to hold a faith which knows tragedy
because it embraces joy, a faith which in tragic realism —
whether or not it avails us with an explanation — always offers and enables a pattern of response.

> The way of the Lord
>   in the womb of the lowly,
> In the greeting of the Spirit
>   for the patience and the travail.
>
> The way of the Lord in the flesh,
>   in the word and the deed,
>   in the path of the Christ.
>
> The oil and the wine in the wound
>   and the pence at the inn,
> The bread and the breaking,
>   The cup and the taking,
>
> In the journey to birth
>   and the wonder of angels.
> In the journey to death
>   and the scars in the hands and the feet —
>
> In the mystery of the readiness of God
>   for the Cross of the world.

CHAPTER 5

A Christ-sharing World

'For us men and for our salvation He came down from heaven . . ? runs the Nicene Creed. A humanity capable of being described inclusively as 'us' is confessed in the context of a conviction about a divine initiative accomplished in Jesus. The sense of a single mankind is expressed almost incidentally in the flow of the credal language. It is not affirmed as some isolated statement of philosophic provenance. It is not a gesture of idealism in the face of vexing particularities of race and place. It comes within a confidence about the self-expression of God in love to a creaturehood of every race and place. But if it is taken in the stride of a sentence about something else, it is by no means incidental to the faith it tells. A universal human-ness is explicit in the incarnate divine-ness Christian faith acknowledged in Jesus as the Christ. It is this simple eloquence of 'us' and 'our' which we have now to examine. Why was it that a theme so distinctive to Jewishness, so private to Jewry, as Messiahship should conceive and make good an intention for the world, that what had been so restrictively 'theirs' should be found to be so impartially ours? And why was it that some of those who had prized Messiah so tenaciously in a corporate isolation from the rest of men came to read Messiah Jesus so insistently as belonging to all?

Such questions belong very closely with the decision shaping Christianity. We have already seen how expanding community was integral to the fact of faith, how it necessitated Gospels as housing its past and renewing its memory, how it required the moral nurture Epistles gave. So doing, those apostolic letters, holding the churches to a common sense of the Church, expressly answered one of the Judaic misgivings about any open 'people of God.' Jewry, for whom, all too often, all other 'peoples were inherently unclean, as corpses are unclean,' (to quote a contemporary Jewish scholar), could not readily risk the claims of the Torah's ethic to the vagaries of the Gentile world. The metaphor of 'pearls before swine' lingered even within the New Testament. Nothing at once sure and pure could be anticipated from the masses in the large world, 'vacant lands and dead people, all of them (to the Temple devotees) an undifferentiated wilderness.'

It was partly on this account that the writers of the Epistles were so assiduous in stressing the personal virtues of social honesty and irreproachable goodness of heart and will. It was not only that the writers knew that the communities, lately recruited from pagan licentiousness or casual living, were prone to irresponsible ways, nor that there was need to curb and educate a restless misreading of the times of God. Their care for the 'imitation' of Christ, studied in the preceding chapter, was practical policy as well as devotional surrender. Paul, above all others, was urgent to re-assure his Jewish friends and critics as to the feasibility of Gentile 'holiness' in those vital ethical areas in which, for the loyal Pharisees, it supremely mattered. On no count can the New Testament be faulted for any indifference to the exacting nature of its task in society because of its universal ambition. Its 'reaching for the world' was no visionary venture mindless of its spiritual liabilities either to Jewish susceptibilities or to Gentile waywardness.

Hence those re-iterated calls, in the Epistles, to a blamelessness which a watching world could recognise and concede to be genuine. Apostles, too, were careful 'to give no offence in anything that the ministry be not blamed.' The sense of a critical scrutiny of individual believers, on the part of a hostile or a cynical world, is everywhere present in the origins of the Christian society. The faith was to be commended in personal integrity of character so that the Messiah identified in Jesus — the Gospel of one who had suffered execution as if he were a malefactor — might stand unashamed both of that paradox and of its peoples' quality. On every count of the Jewish verdict of 'scandal' and the Greek verdict of 'folly' the potential and the proof of Gentile transformation were vital factors in Christian realism about the world. Jewish particularity, for its part, had ample resources of disquiet and scepticism about it, as an enterprise outside the confines of Torah and beyond the frontiers of the holy ground.

It is true that the priestly mind about where sanctity belonged around the sacred mount and the altars of sacrifice was drastically shaken by the capture of Jerusalem under Titus. But, until the desperate failure of the Bar Kokhba revolt sixty-five years later, hopes of the Temple's rebuilding still lingered. In any event the Christian instinct for the wider world had not originated in the tragedy of 70 C.E., though deeply affected by it. When the Rabbis and Sages of Yavneh initiated their courageous re-structuring of the Judaic identity around Torah, study and the synagogue, their embrace of the diaspora condition meant, and required, a still tenacious sense of privacy before God. Though painfully detached from all that tied the priestly temper to a hallowed geography, and though developing what the best in Pharisaism had already envisaged, the holy seed remained intact with the loss of the land. Sage and scribe and student were no less distinctive than the sacrament of place. While the theme of 'wisdom,' alive in Jewry since the return from exile, in measure associated Jewish Torah-consciousness with Persian Greek, Stoic and other thinking, with hints of a universal reason transcending ethnic bounds, it did not diminish the status obtaining between Torah and Jewry. Only the latter had gathered, in all their generations, at Sinai. Only they were parties to the eternal covenant.

It is clear, then, that for all the factors thrusting Jewry into the breadth of the world, whether tragic or congenial, whether the abeyance of Temple ritual or the firm guardianship of Torah, they did nothing to loosen the tenacity of an exclusive identity. It was left to the Christian movement — in which Jewish leadership shared — to give radical and enduring shape to the universality long latent in the Jewish tradition. That the Christian movement availed to do so stems directly and logically from the pattern of Messiahship read from, and in, Jesus by the new community. It is this equation between faith in Jesus and faith for the world which we have to explore. Jewish initiatives within it are vitally

important and sometimes overlooked. No less significant is
how it implemented the rich implications of Jewish vocation and how it was set positively to resolve those tragic
tensions which have so long beset the Jewish condition. They
were tensions sharply present within the New Testament
decision itself and the long centuries of institutional
Christianity have bitterly perpetuated them in perverse
distortion of its own genesis.

Why and how should 'the Christ-shaped story' we have
earlier traced carry us to 'a Christ-sharing world'? The
positive answer can best be reached by some careful, if brief,
review of the way in which things Messianic set Jewry against
the world. For, if priestly Jewry had the sanctuary which
spelled excludedness for others and the Torah-mind had the
law and covenant which did so, Messianic loyalists were
moved to sharpen these into an active belligerence, seeing
humanity at large as inveterate foes.

That temper was fed by bitter resentment at the gathering Roman take-over after the failure of the Maccabees and
the termination of the dubious — and scandalous —
interlude of Herodian vassal-power. What were these
foreigners whose soldiery contrived to subdue the land of
Israel and then, later, to scatter the very people of God from
the vital sanctuary? Did not its defence, and then its recovery,
constitute a prior urgency, since without historical restora-
tion both priest and scribe must be inauthentic? While the
Sages at Yavneh rallied against this reading of history when
Titus had compelled sober minds to a new realism about
current events, the militancy still fired the zeal of zealots.
It was in the-before-and-after of the Fall of Jerusalem
that the Christian version of Messiah-Jesus was steadily
countermanding these stubbornly militant versions of an
authentic 'Son of David.' To appreciate that context for what
it was is to measure how radical was the new faith, how
revolutionary the contrast.

Any lively imagination can register how disconcerting to
Jewish Messianism was this 'Christian' Messiah and how the
contrast turned on reference to the world and the nations.
Messiah, by whatever concept, must undertake a role in
history, act within events and be fulfilled within mankind.

But by what manner of relation to Israel? Was the matrix of the hope to be its exclusive arena? Or, if it was to serve larger than Hebrew ends, on what terms were other peoples to find inclusion — as equal partners both in Messianic blessings and Messianic tasks, or as those whom the blessings eluded and the tasks must subjugate?

As we have seen in chapter 2, Messianic hope had its impulse primarily in the doctrine of creation, in the Creator's responsibility for the human scene in historical time. But from that vital point of departure — without which nothing — the Bible quickly narrowed into the particularity of covenant and Torah. It was there, within Jewish consciousness, that it came to its sharpest focus and was insistently seen as national, Judaic, belonging to Jerusalem and its own. It would have to do with Israel's destiny, with Jerusalem's prosperity, with some final and abiding attainment of the Davidic sovereignty after which it came so often to be named and whose real, or idealised, securities it would re-enact. Other nations might, indeed — on some accounts — share as clients or inferiors in that envisioned rule of Messianic peace, though this dimension faded the more urgent became Israel's need or peril. Whatever might accrue on the margins of the Messianic, its authentic meaning was Judaic, covenantal, ethnic and exclusive.

Yet it is well to note that the Judaic impulses within the Messianic hope had their birth, insistently Judaic as they were, in factors common to all peoples. These, as we saw, were race and land and story — the ethnic identity, the territorial heritage and the historical memory. Did not peoples everywhere give their name to lands or lands to people? Jewish Messianism, both hopefully and tragically, has itself abetted this marriage of destiny between geography and genealogy — a theme to which we must return. But it was there before and independently in many lands and peoples, being — we might say — endemic in human experience. For all have come from a past, around a locale and as a progeny. Nor, in many myths and traditions, is there lacking the conviction of such identity being bestowed by divine favour or mystic warrant, woven into the very texture of existence.

To reckon with this mystique of time and home and womb

as known to all peoples is not to imply that the Hebraic version lacked its own singular intensity and, as many insist, its peculiar warrant. It is to say that what informs the Judaic Messianic belongs with any people, that 'Messiah' cannot finally be privatised as if the yearning that breathes there can be unilaterally fulfilled. It is to say, further, that a Messianic realism must be inclusive. If peace, as we say, is indivisible, can there be a private 'prince of peace'?

We are not hereby saying that the Christian vision of a Messiah for the world sprang from conscious espousal of a general logic. It came from the pattern of Messiahship they believed Jesus to have followed in the conviction of his being 'the Christ of God.' And it had grounds, too, as we must see, in the thoughts within the Hebrew Tanakh, the 'Old Testament' itself. Yet, so coming, it released into all human particularities the option of responding to a peoplehood of vocation, to a reading of identity within a divine providence both of creation and of grace. But it did so, in its New Testament origins, by containing all such segments of the human — as race and place and memory defined them — in a 'household of God' which no identity should annex and in which all might belong. The Jewish identity had been the natal context of that on which an inclusive fulfilment could be freely patterned while itself retaining only the distinction and the tribute of abiding gratitude and perpetual debt.

Thus, it was clearly, with the New Testament, and its insistence on 'We are all one in Christ Jesus,' its repeated doxologies of 'all peoples, nations, tribes and languages standing before the throne of God and of the Lamb.' The union of the sovereignty and the suffering, captured in that graphic clause, alone explains the universal chorus in its celebration. The vision of the Book of Revelation fulfills the promise of Jesus according to John: 'I will draw all men unto me . . . if I be lifted up.' (John 12.32). The universally accessible salvation is that achieved by redeeming love whose price is the Cross.

The Christian decision, then, about Messiahship means that it cannot be unilaterally fulfilled. If the many shapes of birth and land and history are common without ceasing to be particular, and if all ethnic experiences bear marks of providentiality, the ground and structure of hope must be such that all 'the nations bring their glory and their honour into it.' The New Testament saw that the yearning for salvation, explicit in the Jewish theme of Messiah, was out of copyright by the logic of its own genesis in the inter-relation of peoplehood and God. A future for humanity unilaterally vested in the supremcy or presidency of a single people, albeit satisfactory to them, would excite the disquiet of its subject races or instigate their rebellion. Was it not precisely the tolerant Pax Romana against which first century Jewish Messianism was directed? Is it not the central logic of contemporary Zionism that without a land under one's own statehood one cannot be secure and that to be insecure is to be inauthentic? All peoples in their singularity have right to the same logic and these logics, being competitive, will remain at odds with themselves and others and subject to challenge. On these very grounds it has been said, as earlier noted, by Martin Buber, that 'realised Messiahship' is a contradiction in terms. It would seem that the same has to be said about a private Messiahship however realised.

If it was Christianity which perceived the necessity for the world, rather than the nation, as the realm of the Messiah, prophet-seers of Israel had anticipated that Christian vision. How entirely appropriate it was that the first Christians were Jews. For 'the nations' had long been an anxious pre-occupation of the Judaic mind. Deep in the psyche about the land and its story, its Joshuas and Davids, was the sense that what had been acquired at other's expense others could re-acquire to Jewish cost. There was a constant concern — except in the most halcyon days — for the security of tenure in the flux of empires and peoples. Yet, beyond 'the nations' as anxiety-breeders, lay the positive yearning to have them embraced in that 'congratulation' which, from Abraham, they should have reason for because of Israel. Jerusalem should become 'the city of peace' for all mankind, 'all nations flowing into it' in a shared experience of the mercy of Israel's God. Isaiah and Micah heralded the day when 'walking in the light of the Lord,' nations would 'beat their swords into ploughshares' and 'learn war' no more. Amos, too, in his robust dealing with his generation, had insisted that Hebrew Exodus from Egypt had had its parallels in the migrations of Syrians and Philistines (Amos 9.7). The 'Isaiah' of the great 'Servant' passages had made bold to name the Persian Cyrus 'God's anointed' (45.1) and dreamed of 'salvation to the ends of the earth.'

Such passages in the prophetic writings are of one piece with the movement of the New Testament mind. They were far from being, except at times with Amos, the rhetoric of rebuke to overweening Jewry from a God who also had His Ethiopians and Persians. They were beyond such prophet-tactics and belonged with an urgent sense that covenantal exceptionality could not, and should not, write off the world but must somehow and somewhere translate into its wideness. For — if we may paraphrase John Wesley — 'a solitary salvation' in denying the world for its parish denied itself as salvation. These voices in the Hebrew Tanakh are kin with the apostles of the New Testament in the geography of faith.

But, in resolving whether Messiah would be against the nations as foes or for them as recruits, the heirs of the covenant sensed a deep dilemma. Did not universality turn necessarily on an uncompromising particularity? Was it not for the world's own sake that Jews must never abandon or surrender their specialness with God? Thus all the noble instincts towards the wider world required a steady exemption from it. Jewry could only be self-expending on behalf of the nations in remaining self-reserving from them. It was precisely this dilemma which the New Testament overcame by transferring the instrumental peoplehood from the realm of nation-people-covenant consciousness into a peoplehood constituted on the sole principle of faith and gathered out of any and every culture, any and every tribe. Any such radical revision of Messiah-in-his-people proved impossible to the Jewish mind as involving a forfeiture of that very identity — their identity under God — within which alone a Messianic meaning could transpire. Salvation for the world would be nullified without the safeguarding of the private entity which conditioned it.

Thus it was that even in the most generous moments of

care for the nations Jewishness withheld, for the nations' sake, its own self-oblation. This takes us to the very core of the New Testament decision. 'The household of God' was not merely to have a mind for the world: it was to be born in generations of diversity. Universality as the Church intended it could be unreserving because its Messiah had ended the case for reservations — those reservations which had checked the finest instincts of the prophets and sustained the wildest instincts of the Zealots.

It was little wonder that a change so drastic as that explicit in the *new* testament should occasion bitter resentment within the old order and entail deep stresses for those, like Paul, finding their way through its toll on the emotions and on outward relationships. Something of those strains on heart and mind are evident in Paul's struggle, in Romans 9 to 11, to conserve Judaic identity and affirm a universal church. He wants to see the divine destiny for Israel consummated in a new community where the Jew/Gentile distinction is obsolete. But he also wants to feel that 'the gift and calling of God are without repentance', that is, remain unchanged. The impasse latent here between an ongoing covenant of single provenance and an open covenant of grace has never been resolved.

Perhaps Paul's ambivalence is the only tolerable 'solution', given all that Jewry has since suffered by its fidelity — suffering to which the people of open grace have vastly and tragically contributed. Perhaps, though incompatible, we have to hold together an Abrahamic/Mosaic covenant never meant for any open grace fulfilment and its open grace fulfilment which actually happened. To do so would at least be to recognise that, where religious convictions are concerned, a faith in faith is their *de facto* warrant, leaving 'absolutes' of truth, not to contention, but to silence. If so, it will be a silence about foreclosing a contradiction, not a silence about embracing an inclusive divine love within creation where there is only the 'us' and 'our' of a human whole. It must be for us a silence in which gratefully to cherish, not tacitly to ignore, the Christian decision.

For that decision has abiding import both for Jews and non-Jews. Has not the 'chosen people' concept been responsible for sad and tragic consequences in human history? Within Jewry, as their own mentors have struggled to correct, it has generated an insistent pre-occupation with the attitude of others. It has at times become an almost neurotic suspicion of the world at large. It has always required its due recognition. For its meaning turned not only on interior conviction but on external concession of its truth. Lacking this, in what would its psychic significance consist? Like the subjective idealist's view of objects in philosophy, 'its being was to be perceived.' Anxiety supervened when such necessary perception of the unique status was lacking or, more painfully still, was denied.

What should we say of this tragic situation in which the claim to divine specialness ethnically enjoyed excites its own rejection? History darkly re-enacts the crime of Joseph's brothers. He alone had 'the coat of many colours,' with Jacob's over-fond indulgence. They were only Leah's sons, not Rachel's or they were baser born to serving maids. Their revengeful anger can have no exoneration and anti-Semitism remains a grievous, heinous crime. But should we understand the very economy of God by the analogy of Jacob's love for Joseph? Or do we know what tribal strains and enmities lie behind the patriarchal narratives with rejection of the Esaus and the Ishmaels in the interests of the 'chosen'? There were, to be sure, providences in Joseph's dreams and story which the brothers came to acknowledge. But the agony of Jacob persists in what history crudely calls 'the Jewish question.' Can it merely be coincidence that the world's most insistently 'different' community has been historically the most desperately persecuted?

The persecutors are in no way absolved. Nor does the question mean to conceal the shame belonging to Christian factors aiding and abetting the persecutors. Yet the more we align (as a book title has it) 'faith and fratricide' the more are we involved in the enigma of the exclusive covenant, of faith and non-fraternity. For non-fraternity is implicit, and sometimes, explicit in the Judaic definition of 'the Gentiles,' who were not at Sinai. If we as Christians hold the Old and

New Testaments (as we describe them) to be rightly within a single Bible, then we acknowledge Judaic 'chosen peoplehood' to be divine wisdom on the way to open grace. Could it be divine wisdom if not so opened?

No doubt we can escape the pain of this question if we fall back on the arbitrary finality which simply affirms: 'God chose the Jews.' When we do so we of course ignore the protest of many modern Jews, like David Ben Gurion of renewed Zion, that it was in fact Jews who 'chose God' in the resilience of their own self-guided destiny. But that aside, any such foreclosing of all that is at issue, in a simple assertion of 'election,' ignores the gnawing doubt as to whether divine ways can be seen as sheer arbitrariness not warranted by larger moral ends. Must we not assume, about God, a purposiveness of undifferentiating love? Otherwise how do we refute a cynic's scepticism about chosenness as no more than a virile version of identity? If 'election' is not to be, as deriders allege, an astute form of tribal self-image, a confidence trick of leadership, or a way of reading the drama of one's history, it must surely be a means to an end beyond itself. Christian faith repudiates and condemns all those cynical calumnies. It gratefully salutes an authentic chosenness, finding it authentic in being the pathway of a Messiah for the world.

Such gratitude has cause to wonder deeply about the long travail of the continuing chosenness which does not see itself vindicated in those Christian terms, realising how tragic, both in physical and psychic ways, Jewish travail has been. Faith in a realised Messiahship must mean faith in a fulfilled Jewishness — fulfilled, not abrogated. How, then, can such faith interpret the continuing profound Jewish non-abrogation standing impressively in refusal to be so fulfilled? The question is all the sharper in that Chistian history contains so deep and dark an antagonism to Jewish fidelity. Persecution of Jewry at the hands of Christian perversity has so grimly compromised the faith that had translated chosenness into openness to all.

Anguish belongs not only in what others have done against the Jews. It lies also in what others have done in their imitation. The 'chosen people' concept has been tragically

emulated and invoked from Leningrad to Pretoria, from
Byzantium to the new world, from the Middle Ages to the
present day. Given the ways of human nature, to guess at
'election' can be a contagious thought. Cromwell hails his
victory at Marston Moor where 'deliverance was the Lord's'
and makes massacre in Ireland fortified by the Book of
Psalms. Providences like the Exodus can be read into the
great trek of the Boers across the Vaal. There are other rivers
than Jordan beyond which there are 'heathen' fit to be
subdued by 'captains of the Lord of hosts.' Any lust of place
and power can clothe itself in divine legitimacy.

The Jews themselves have so often and so tragically been
the victims of such delusions on the part of Aryans, and
others. 'Blood, Fatherland and Volk', devised the Holocaust.
Some of the most virulent forms of anti-Semitism lie at the
door of 'chosenness.' Witness Dostoevsky for whom there
could be only one 'chosen people' — they of 'holy Russia.'
Such notions are bound to be intolerant, for there can be no
competitors, the mystique being then forfeited. These dark
emulations of 'chosen' status are all too readily politicized.
Political Zionism this century has itself set the example in
that a mystique of destiny and of supernatural legitimacy
has been deftly recruited to practical state-building and
diplomacy on that behalf. It is revealing that in the trauma
of the seventies and the eighties in the Lebanon some in
the Maronite community have been stimulated, openly or
sub-consciously, by Israel to conceive their stake in the land
by comparable rubric of 'election under God' and so to
emulate Zionist prowess in confronting forces arrayed against
them — forces which in that context can be read as the same.

There is a sense, on the broad scene and in the long tale
of history, that such politicizing is inevitable where the theme
of destiny obtains. It carries a presumption of sanction for
whatever is necessary, a heightened sense of 'us' and 'them'
and a determination not to be impugned. The reader of the
Psalms, for all their tender devotion, can often register this
climate of harsh encounter, a temper that has identified God's
enemies in the psalmist's own. Can we doubt that the peril
in the thought of 'chosenness' may well be more active than
the benediction? At their best and finest, are physical

peoplehood, and ethnic identity, consolidated in land and power and state, well calculated to carry unilateral entrustment with divine ends? At their worst must they not surely impede and distort them?

Nowhere is that misgiving more eloquently confirmed than in the contrasted self-image of Jewry in the long diaspora. To be sure, the ethnic, religious dimension endured as the crux of all else. But 'chosenness' was then made good in powerlessness, in gentleness and fidelity, in patient presence among the nations, in sufferance and pain. In all these ways, as in the circumstance of dispersion *per se*, it resembled closely the New Testament understanding of the Church, save for the necessity of Jewish birth. The Church, too, was scattered, and vulnerable, with no native land yet everywhere 'native.' It believed, as did many in diaspora Judaism, that its condition, precarious and vexing, nevertheless enabled it to fulfill its vocation to the world. Only when it succumbed to the blandishments of power, or allowed itself to be annexed by nationality and empire, did it forfeit its founding quality and obscure the intention of its origin. There are those who would see in political Zionism something of the same forfeiture of self-understanding by diaspora Judaism, whereby the State of Israel has renewed all the tragic ambiguities of divine election.

To enlist the significance of diaspora Jewry to illumine the natal character of the Church and to ponder the tensions 'chosenness' incurs, is not to imply that the Christian decision for 'a Christ-sharing world' derived from such conscious reasoning. It was not born in analytical reflection. It followed from the sort of Messiah Jesus had been or — anticipating our later query — as 'Christians' believed him to have been. For Messiah-Jesus satisfied no zealot and launched no nation-state. There was about his teaching a realism which did not differentiate human nature, as to the thrust of evil, or the hope of good, by reference to birth or to 'election'. Even of stones God was able to 'raise up children to Abraham.' Jesus deliberately pictured Samaritans as 'good' and 'grateful,' refusing routine disdain of the 'low born.' He detected and evoked faith in the most unlikely quarters. His whole moral emphasis ignored the prejudice, the niceties,

of people-pride and fastidious Torah-scruple. How refreshing
it was to be with Jesus on the Sabbath.

Luke among the evangelists captures this openness in that
deceptively simple phrasing in the parables: 'Now a certain
man . . .' There is no need to differentiate or identify. Rich
fools or grieving fathers do not need to be labelled Jew or
Gentile. Owners of lost sheep or lost silver are likely to behave
in the same manner, searching the terrain or sweeping the
floors. Even where culture varies the setting, the impulses
are one and human. Jesus knew the physical limits of his
mission among 'the lost sheep of the house of Israel,' but
there were no limits to the reach and relevance of his
Beatitudes. The children of Abraham would have to share
with east and west, with north and south, in the community
of 'the kingdom of heaven.' While there may be scholarly
debate about Jesus' intention for the world there can be no
doubt that the theme and temper of his invitation to his
hearers sought and found them in simply human terms.
Where the Gospels sound ambivalent about Jewish privilege
it is because their composition took shape within the throes
of the decision we are studying.

But the 'drawing of all mankind' had to do supremely with
the pattern of the Cross. That climax, its antecedents and
its sequel, disowned the demands of national ardour. Its
anguish had to do, not with the yoke of Rome but with 'the
sin of the world.' Pilate's trial-question: 'So you are a king
then?' was answered in the crown of thorns. Bystanders
thought Jesus was 'calling for Elijah.' But here was no massacre
of the prophets of Baal. The zealot-brigands on either side,
according to Luke, represented the burning issue between
inveterate violence and its final repudiation. Luke is clear
how and why it was that Jesus for ever resolved that issue
in words exchanged that day.

Early Christian imagery saw in the *ekpetasis,* the arms
stretched upon the Cross, the gesture of embrace, an embrace
of the world. It was the human whole which God, they said,
'so loved.' Had the merit of the law sufficed the Cross would
have been unnecessary as redemption. But, by the same
token, it would not have occurred as an event. For was not
the will to crucify a crucial index to the wrongness of

mankind? (There is point in the associated words). It is well to realise that the teaching career of Jesus was in no way a resounding success. People may have been impressed, gladdened, even enthused. But the way was hard, the honesty disconcerting and the establishment entrenched. There was a descending spiral of rejection, a hardening of the heart, an evaporation of enthusiasm. The final factors were no doubt conspiratorial, concerting the climax to forestall sympathy and to counter popular support, counting on how fickle or casual popular support would be. In the event some at least of the populace were readily recruited for the outcome. In a variety of ways, whether of action or inaction, it is evident how the Cross of Jesus accuses human society alike in its religious mentors, its political masters and its common folk.

It is therefore evident also how the Cross accomplishes a Messiahship engaged in no narrow enterprise of national vindication or recovery of ethnic pride, a Messiahship standing in the virtue of a love that suffers. It refuses the victories of violence that are always partial, exclusive, impermanent and stained, victories which see enemies to eliminate not enmities to redeem, victories which by their nature exclude, if they do not liquidate, their foes, victories which only change the name or seat of evil. Those other, legitimate occasions of considerate power it does not comprehend as Messianic. For, politically valid, even laudable, as they may be, there are reaches of human need — for forgiveness, mercy, grace and hope — which they can never attain. There is that within us for which only love suffices and the love that suffices for it must always suffer to suffice. So it is, by Christian decision of faith, with God.

Therefore, a Christ-sharing world it had to be. 'Go and make disciples of all nations' (Matt. 28.19) was understood to be Jesus' watchword for his community. What is called 'the great commission,' as we have seen, became a conscious mandate in the doing and the going. As they went they were aware of being sent. The Gospel they had discovered could not be realised in privacy or in seclusion. It demanded to be told. It had not been constituted in divine reservation from the human whole. It must, therefore, be unreservedly given to mankind. When the disciples listened, out of all their experience, to the Jesus in whom they read the Christ, they heard him to have said: 'I came to save the world.' (John 12.47), and that sufficed them.

Jerusalem remained the loved locale of the party among them staunch to its centrality in tradition and awesome affection. But — probably by the impetus of Stephen, the first martyr — outreach became the steady impulse of a venturing faith. Luke certainly wrote in the warmth of that enthusiasm. Some suspect that he idealised the role of Rome, and it may well be that there were factors of reluctance, deserving our attention, of which we have not heard. Jerusalem and Judaic tradition were tenacious of their honour. The city's calling to be 'the mother of us all' was a hard vocation for her proper children. Historians need an ear for silences.

Yet, in the event, those 'uttermost parts' — as they were only by Mediterranean measure — both comforted and admonished Jerusalem when they rallied to her material need. The 'Gentile offertory,' which played so decisive a role in Paul's career, was a significant transaction in the shared Messiah, a sacrament of diversity in unity. It was in Antioch, the base of missionary extension, that 'Christians' according to Luke (Acts 11.26), first received that name. Their very identity and the term that captured it coincided with their will for humanity.

To be alive to this intention for the world is to face the disconcerting fact that its documentation in the New Testament is confined to the westward direction. Those maps which serve the study of the apostles are all trans-Mediterranean. Like the inscription over Jesus' Cross the languages are 'Hebrew, Greek and Latin.' The faith is told in the speech in which it was first placarded. Tradition may take Mark to Egypt, Thaddeus to Armenia, Thomas to India, but their narratives have no status in holy writ. The New Testament Canon confines itself to Asia Minor and Europe. It is a situation logic requires us to deplore. And more than logic. For how such south-bound, east-bound, Christians encountered the Hindu, the Buddhist or the African would be a story well suited to the trust of the faith, not to say its task today. Only one questioner of the travelling Church survives in the record away from the Mediterranean. His puzzlement, as an Ethiopian, about 'the lamb' and the prophet and the text, does solitary duty for all that the mind of Asia had — and still has — to interrogate about what reaches it in Christian 'Hebrew, Greek and Latin.'

This unresolved question concerning the New Testament's documentary partiality in the task of a faith mandated to the world is one we have to live with. But as least we have the precedents that belonged in 'Hebrew, Greek and Latin.' Duties of interpretation outside those languages of faith's explicit origins are sterner and wider. Nor is the Holy Spirit circumscribed by apostolic circuits whether of place or culture. Whether it be Paul on Mars Hill, or John of Ephesus in that Aegean capital, or Luke in presentation for Theophilus, the hints are discernible about how it might be done elsewhere. To have the ambition of a Christ-sharing world means to hold a Christ whom none can monopolise, alive to a world which no faith monopolises. We have vastly more reason to appreciate that double fact in our time than the apostles had in theirs. Articulate co-existence and the inter-penetration of societies and cultures are the pattern of our contemporary situation. It is precisely because there has to be, on the part of the religions, a conscious sharing of the world that the distinctive heart of Christianity must inform that consciousness.

According to old Jewish tradition the voice which spoke on Sinai was heard as if coming from all four corners of the world, from north, south, east and west, as the people turned around to hear. We should not think differently of the voice that sounds in the word of the Gospel. It is given into particular trust, into a peoplehood of faith and fellowship. But they hear it on behalf of the whole compass of mankind. Christ-loyalty has to be world-loyalty.

It follows that a Christ who cannot be ours except in being also the world's entails a faith which cannot be secured from the world. Only in a readiness to be doubted can it deserve to be trusted. Hence the two chapters to come.

CHAPTER 6

Questions Ever Present

'The Church has words . . . modern man has questions,' writes a recent newspaper editorial commenting on a human tragedy. Why 'modern'? Interrogating the faith did not begin yesterday, Nor are words all that the Church has. It has the Christ. Questions too have words, or they could not be heard. What matters is the worth, the drift, of our transactions with them. A faith about the real world, and turning on events in history, could hardly find its genesis, nor sustain its meaning, nor survive its centuries, without the summons to reply, on this score and on that, to the queries or misgivings which attend it like birds behind the plough. For the ground it breaks in holding what it does excites a curiosity or a scepticism drawn towards the furrows that it leaves. Faith, in that sense, sets the arena for doubt, occupies it with its own agenda when, otherwise, the dubious would find themselves differently engaged.

It has been implicit through the foregoing chapters that this is peculiarly so with Christianity. Where question is most concentrated is precisely where conviction is most germinal, namely in the Christian verdict as to the Christ and the Christ factor in the Christian. This we saw at the outset in taking 'the Christian(s)' as the mediating term between Christ and Christianity. Had 'they' rightly known 'him'? Or, putting the question differently: 'Who shaped who in their own image? Were the first Christians dependably such by a Jesus who was as they took him to have been? Or was what they took him to have been the mistaken reading of a community generating themselves in the process around an illusion, or at least a confusion, a fervour which cold history will not sustain?

There can be no doubt that this is the vital issue. It might simply be left to turn on the query: Which is the more

worthy of credence, or the less worthy of doubt: that Jesus
as the Christ originated the faith that made the apostles, or
that the disciples originated the faith that made him the
Christ? But sceptics may feel that such a formula loads the
dice too heavily against them. For their sake let the issue have
more subtle exploration. We need to look searchingly at the
considerations which might have availed to tempt or goad
or misguide the disciples into the cumulative decision about
Jesus and Messiahship which allegedly distorted the Jesus
of history into the Christ of faith. What might those factors
have been? Where will honesty with them leave the issue in
the end? What will they mean for the mettle of the faith that
gives them hearing?

We should first exclude the wild surmises about Passover
plots and Messianic legacies that savour more of oppor-
tunistic journalism than credible scholarship. The notion
that the evangelists — albeit perhaps faulted in this or that
— practised a deliberate duplicity cannot square with the
crystal sincerity which breathes through both Gospels and
Epistles in the New Testament. They certainly proceeded
upon a meaning — a meaning turning on a personality and
deriving from an event. What warrants faith or suggests doubt
was not, either way, a fraud or a deception. There was a Jesus
and there came a church: there was a cross and there came
a gospel. Did what eventuated enshrine the event? Did the
meaning authorise the apostles, making them such? Or did
the disciples author the meaning mistaking it so?

A will to integrity about this issue will naturally enquire
whether there were any discernible factors present which
might have prompted the first Christians into what we can
now see to have been a distortion, a misconstruing of Jesus.
The obvious candidate for such a role would be the pagan
traditions of redeemer-gods descending from above for the
rescue of humanity. As noted earlier, such notions of celestial
bearings on things mundane stemmed from the influence
of the gnostics of those first Christian centuries. For
gnosticism abounded in esoteric cults in which disciples
savoured mysteries hidden from outsiders, mysteries having
to do with heavenly visitants only apparently embodied in
human shape and proposing eternal salvation to their

votaries on the basis of cultic devotion focussed in celebratory rites. Some observers have found associations here with the Christian Eucharist and have alleged approximations to them in some of the language of the Epistles. We recall too that Roman Emperors were regularly deified and translated to the pantheon of the heavens. Could these Graeco-Roman pagan sources give their clue to the flights — as such critics would see them — of Christian Christology?

Our purpose here is not to set up a series of targets which we then shoot down with reassuringly dismissive speed. Let us leave the sceptics to be simplistically dismissive of the faith: the truth is never facile. Christian decision had its environment and could not otherwise have related to this world and, therefore, not to Jesus. The question for us is whether environment accounts for the faith or whether the faith reacts to environment. We need a care here about chronology. Some theories of gnostic influences, as well as Jewish controversy, assume as present what in fact post-dated the New Testament. Within the right time-range its writers, as we have seen, were alert and resistant.

One ruling consideration in this context must be the fact that the Christian decision about Jesus was emphatically the decision of Jews, rooted — as Jews would feel only Jews could be — in unyielding monotheism. Greatly as we must acknowledge and admire the resilient relationship with the Greek tradition achieved by such a figure as Philo of Alexandria, it is clear that the eternal *Shema:* 'Hear, O Israel, our Lord, the Lord is One' regulated all such associations with Hellenism. It was within this staunch confession of 'the only Lord' that the faith about Jesus as divine originated and with which it struggled to be for ever consistent. Hence, later, the careful definitions and the doctrine of the Trinity in the new understanding of God as credibly and redemptively One. On this vital score there is hardly a balance of credibility in favour of an interpretation of Jesus being owed to pagan, gnostic factors disorienting a Jewish community in the understanding of a divine saviour.

It has been inferred by some readers of the New Testament, and of the Acts in particular, that a Christology of Jesus at

Jewish hands arose from a need to cancel out the shame of crucifixion — a cancelling for which the Resurrection was the warrant. Jesus was somehow Messiah in spite of the ignominy of death on a cross and the routine malediction about 'the curse of hanging on a tree.' (Deut. 21.23, Gal. 3.13) Faith needed the dimension of glory to offset the anathema, so faith opted for his exaltation to 'the right hand of God' on high, having no heart for an abiding crucifix.

But, whatever the place of the crucifix in piety, this is to pervert the entire emphasis of New Testament believing. As we have seen, the Resurrection does not make amends for a tragedy. It ensues upon love's triumph and love's triumph is with the Cross and not in spite of it. The glory into which Gospels and Epistles alike understand Jesus to have entered is inseparable from the shame. For by the paradox of grace the shame is the very point where the glory transpires. It would be an odd perception of theology, or of Jesus, to read New Testament Christology as compensation for defeat or as obviating a scandal. There was no defeat on Calvary and the scandal itself was the confidence of the Gospel.

Keeping within the Jewish milieu here, before returning to the gnostic issue, the question arises whether the Gospel about Jesus' suffering as an event within the being of God can be traced to the Akedah, the sacrifice of Isaac by Abraham in the Genesis story? Could this have been a matrix of a Jewish Christology? It would seem not. The term Akedah is not used in Scripture and its emergence in Jewish midrash would seem to be no earlier than the second century C.E. when all hope of a resumption of Temple sacrifices after the collapse of Bar Kokhba's revolt had to be abandoned. Nor is the testing of Abraham in any way analogous with what Christians understood to be enacted in Jesus. Where Paul, in Romans 8.32, might seem to come closest to it, in: 'He that spared not His own Son...' there is no mention of Isaac. Rabbinic exegesis of Isaac followed very different lines from Christian interpretation of the Cross. Nowhere is the story in Gen. 22 used as a prototype of Messiah. It would seem that Christian decision about the redeeming quality of Jesus' suffering arose from within convictions of his 'sonship' and Messianic servanthood deriving from prophetic precedent

and interpreted out of Jesus' own consciousness as read by
the disciples post-resurrection. In becoming apostles, those
disciples had the act of Jesus' Gethsemane as the source of
their mind about suffering and the clue to Messianic identity.

But when the 'sonship' theme latent in Messiahship within
the Hebraic tradition passes into the 'Sonship' that is the
very 'exegesis' of God, from 'the bosom of the Father' (John
1.18), what then? Is the movement from 'the one mind with
the Father' which is active obedience, into 'the one mind'
which is unity of being, credibly attributable to the
undoubted presence of gnostic teaching in the setting of the
early Church? For many the temptation to think so has been
strong. Yet, for all the features of first Christian cultic and
intellectual life that betray resemblances to those of
gnosticism, there remains one pre-eminent consideration
against deriving the one from the other — the constant
affirmation of the historical actuality of 'the Word made
flesh.'

Terms borrowed from gnosticism, like 'mystery' and
being 'initiated into the secret' might find their way into
Christian vocabulary and even become central to the
expression of Christian experience. Indeed there have been
those who have suspected the Fourth Gospel as being itself
a 'gnostic' writing — though others, paradoxically, have seen
its purpose as being precisely the repudiation of gnosticism.
This divided mind of the learned is only symptomatic of how
apostolic faith moved vitally in and with its environment.
But there can be no doubt where the verdict must lie about
the Johannine position on this score. For, at the heart of
gnosticism, was the disavowal of the body and all its
compromise of pure spirit enmeshed in 'the flesh.' Hence
the heresy which distressed the sub-apostolic age, if not New
Testament times also, for which the divine-ness of Jesus had
to require that his physicality was no more than apparent,
that his history — and most of all his death on the Cross
— was a sort of charade, a 'seeming' that had not really
'occurred.'

To believe that, on the contrary, the earthly life and history
of the actual Jesus had been 'in the flesh' the very expression of God was to part company totally with gnostic

immunity. John's imagery of 'the tent spread among us' (John 1.14) might perversely be made to imply some kind of illusory transience, some kind of insubtantial 'make-believe.' But the verb has no such ambience. It belongs squarely with the Hebraic theme of the 'tabernacle' in the wilderness, the Shechinah or 'presence,' in which God was believed to accompany, indeed to escort, the actual journeyings of the people. There is no evasion of time or place or circumstance here. For it is these, precisely, which are the stuff of revelation and the fabric of meaning.

When gnostics came to write gospels they were wildly different from those of the four Evangelists. There is nothing gnostic about the urgent down-to-earth eventfulness of Mark with milling crowds and vociferous beggars and eager hands breaking up the roof overhead. While the evangelists, to a man, are reverently reticent about the physical pathos of the Cross there is no mistaking the bitter actuality of nails and spear and blood. And, as we have earlier seen, they tell of a real tomb and a grim burial and of a Roman governor surprised at the victim's less than lingering demise. However we decide to interpret the presentation of Jesus' risen appearances, it is to this intense realism of Golgotha and the grave that we must link them as the form of the disciples' persuasion of his victory. John is no less immersed in this concreteness of events than his fellow writers and in his Epistles is insistent that it is crucial to 'confess that Jesus *is* come in the flesh.'

When the early Church came — if we may so speak — to Latinise its credal terms it was just this 'substantial' emphasis which it introduced into its formula: 'Of one substance with the Father.' There is a subtlety about its technical sense and it is one which modern philosophical thought has left behind. But there is point in its image even so. For that which stands under the divine self-disclosure is the living flesh and blood of human biography. Conversely what that actual history conveys can be trusted as the authentic exposition of the nature of God. When Christmas piety sings of 'veiled in flesh the Godhead see' it can rightly mean no illusoriness, only the paradox, not of a disguise, but of a disconcerting presence, the veil as a means to sight and not its denial.

One can, therefore, scarcely think the Christian witness about Jesus as the Christ to have derived from gnostic depreciation or abhorrence of 'the flesh,' seeing that their Gospel prized it so highly on account of who and how Jesus had been indwelling it. The faith had much more to do, as we hinted in chapter 2, with the way in which the personality of prophets had pointed forward to how 'words uttered' on behalf of God might become 'a word' biographised, how spokesmen for God might become, in measure, the embodiment, in fidelity and suffering, of the truth they served in the travail of telling it. So it had been with Amos and with Jeremiah as bearers of 'truth in personality,' lending the dynamic of who they were to the impact of what they said. For all its distinctiveness in the Christian tradition, the apostolic witness to Jesus stands in clear continuity with such prophetic precedent. The thought that the divine could be explicit in the human, not only on the tongue but in the character, not merely by the voice but through the self, has far surer affinity with the Hebrew heritage of prophethood than with the tenuous and devious associations of the gnostics.

Furthermore, the Greek and Egyptian concepts of dying and rising 'saviours,' current in the Mediterranean milieu, involve no convincing compatibility with what was affirmed about Jesus. Osiris, Adonis, Attis and Mithras played their part in mystic cults and celebratory rituals as objects of veneration for the salvations they proferred. What the first Christians understood about Jesus, in the grimly historical reality of Jerusalem's place of execution, was that his death itself had redeeming significance for each and all, not for a privacy of devotees. Those cult figures, in the Mysteries, did not redeem by their suffering: it was they themselves who were retrieved from mourning by return to life, a return which might then release emotions of happiness and hope. What obtained in Jesus was a self-oblation having its interpretation through the traditions of Hebraic prophethood.

To stress in this way the strong Hebraic antecedents of Christian decision and its Jewish making is not to ignore the Gentile factor. Non-Jews had their positive share in the shaping of the faith and its vocabulary. It is clear, too, that Gentile predilections entailed the Church in many tensions, some of which are evident within the New Testament writings, not least in the Letter to the Colossians and the Pastoral Epistles. It is the very fact of these struggles with actual or potential distortion of the Christian meaning from the Gentile world and pagan religion which attests the will to loyalty within Hebraic origins. The equal welcome the new faith had for diverse peoples, believed to be incorporate with Israelites in Christ, did not mean any careless hospitality to their old assumptions. On the contrary, the New Testament insisted throughout on the exclusive authority of 'Christ Jesus' as the very crux of loyalty to the monotheism of historic Jewry. In renouncing any ethnic exclusivism they had no room for an inclusivism that would betray the Oneness of the God they had learned from Abraham, Moses and the prophets and Whom they believed they had truly encountered in the event of Jesus. If we are to see the New Testament portrayal of Jesus as in any sense a 'Hellenising' of his significance it happened strictly within the context of interpreting and sharing the reach of his Hebraic Messiahship. There was a commending, not a forfeiting, of identity in the relation of the new faith to the new environment of Greece and Rome. That conclusion seems more impressive than the conjectures we have been exploring for which extraneous influences beguiled the Church into a Christ no longer according to Jesus.

We must now, however, turn this whole situation around. The alleged 'Hellenising' of Jesus needs, to be sure, more detail than we have allowed it. But we can make some amends for this — and usefully to the main concern — if we examine what some would call the 're-Judaising' of Jesus. How do the questions look if we ponder them from the Galilean end — or rather the Galilean beginning? Let us move back from the Christ of the New Testament faith to Jesus the Jew of Nazareth and ask what aberration there has been. Was he not a would-be rabbi, a teacher, a wandering healer with charismatic powers and a fleeting popular following? May it not be said that much in his verbal teaching could be found elsewhere in the wisdom of the 'liberal' Pharisees? If there

was any decision from which Christianity derived must it
not have been an admiration for, a determination to
commend, the Sermon on the Mount? It is surely from his
words, rather than from abstractions allegedly about 'the
Word,' that Jesus must be understood and followed.

This position, variously formulated of old and of late,
appeals to many in contemporary agnosticism about credal
'extravagance.' It is also in line with much Jewish scholarship
now amply overtaking its long inhibition of neglect about
the Christians' Jesus, whom it saw as either renegade or
irretrievably pre-possessed by Rome, Byzantium, Geneva and
the rest. It also suits the instincts of Islam, where Jesus is
God's 'messenger,' no more, an illustrious predecessor to
Muhammad in a long line of 'apostles' in the sequence from
a God Who mercifully 'sends' but never 'comes,' a God for
Whom the 'compromise' of Incarnation is impossible. Let
us have the Jesus who was the mouthpiece of a divine wisdom,
the 'teacher of righteousness' whose authority stands in the
sheer truth of noble utterance, not in the pseudo-status of
a misguided Christology. Let us reverse the excesses of those
who, in the language of the Irish poet, 'swept the sawdust
from the floor of that working carpenter,' in a mistaken will
to endow Jesus with an aura he never sought and must for
ever have repudiated. Let us, with Muslims and Jews and
others, 'undeify' Jesus and return, disencumbered of
Christology, to the fresh air of Galilee.

Historic Christianity, believing it has never forsaken
Galilee, does well to attend keenly to such exhortation. For
there would have been no Cross outside the gate had there
been no Sermon on the Mount. The historic faith means
no neglect of the spoken word, no inattention to the prophet-
teacher. While it is true, as liberation theologians realise, that
speculative Christology *may* preclude obedience to moral
demands, there is no proper, or necessary, cleavage between
'words' and 'the Word.' It was, after all, the faith which wrote
the Gospels and had an urgency to do so because it treasured
all that Jesus had said. 'That which we have seen, and heard
and handled...' (1 John 1.1) was how one of the New
Testament writers referred back to the experience of actual
history as memory recalled it, and he was one of the most

insistent of theologians of 'the Christ.' Throughout in the Epistles, as we saw in chapter 4, there is no indifference to 'the messenger' Jesus, rather a haunting reverberation of his message. In the articulate faith there was always this hyphen of love between 'Jesus' and 'Christ' in their speech and thought.

So the strange paradox is that it is precisely to the faith making Christology that we owe the transcript of the teaching. Without the 'aura' which some wish to subtract in the alleged interest of 'simplicity,' it is certain we would have no survival of the words from Galilee. The community which treasured them, echoed them in its pastoral education, and rehearsed them in its fellowship, was the sole agent of their transmission to the centuries. Without that recalling and recording aegis, the aegis of faith in Christ, posterity would have known the barest minimum of the wisdom of Jesus, if any at all. This is a paradox which those who discount or denigrate the faith they see as oddly elaborated, do well to recognise.

But there is a deeper paradox still. It has to do with the manifest non-success of that teaching, as teaching in the human scene of its time and place. As the Gospels see it, the career of Jesus was not a gathering climax of recognition and acclaim. There was no way to greatness on the wings of oratory after the manner of Demosthenes, or Cicero. We find, not a crescendo of applause, but a denouement into crucifixion. The question for us is not only how 'good' the teaching was but how 'bad' it proved the world to be. Its reception was no less significant than its content. The historic faith did right to reckon with this daunting actuality of Jesus' rejection. Not that doing so it abandoned what he taught about love, gentleness, mercy and purity of heart, but because these had to make their way in a world minded to impale them on a cross. That history threw his disciples back upon a realism for which a cherished wisdom had to be served and told within a perspective that could incorporate the tragic climax of its unforgettable expression. This is where Christology originates, in a painful reckoning with the tragedy of human wrong — a wrong in mind and will which teaching indicted not merely by what it affirmed but by how it suffered. If we want a moralism which is without illusion we had better seek it from the lips of Jesus and find it around the Cross of Christ. It is in those terms that there is no forgetting Galilee.

But wait, say those who would isolate Jesus' ethic and dissociate it from historic faith and creeds. His teaching is not to be so readily overwhelmed in tragedy. We need not incriminate the world quite so desperately. His teaching need not be tied quite so closely to the implications of his death. What transpired may perhaps be interpreted as a tragic accident, an unfortunate coincidence of circumstances — a high priesthood set on the prudence of expediency, a governor liable to indecision and callous in resolving it, a volatile mob kindled into easy frenzy. And what if the prisoner himself somehow precipitated his end, or Judas did so, in expectation of a cataclysmic intervention from on high? With all these factors present, need we be discouraged about the durability, nevertheless, of what the victim left behind in word and quality?

Perhaps. But who would have route-d that legacy to us had there been no believers in his total relevance, no worshippers around 'the Throne of God *and* of the Lamb'? The Sermon on the Mount was not to be so painlessly bequeathed. Moreover, was there not a wholeness about Jesus in that his teaching and his Messianic vocation, as sensed and suffered, were all of one piece, a seamless robe? There need be no sundering of prelude and climax. Nazareth was itself placarded on the Cross. Jesus suffered as he taught and taught as he suffered. It was not only that the Cross was consequential upon his teachng in our sort of world, it was also consistent with the content in his sense of truth. It was 'the cup my Father has given me' in being the price of 'your heavenly Father knows . . ' This wholeness in the ministry of Jesus — if we follow the Gospels — excludes the possibility of a deliberate gamble to induce apocalyptic intervention from on high or any other theories of Jesus' intentions in Gethsemane. Had these been a gambler's or a suicide's or a desperado's, would they not have deprived us of the teaching also?

'If we follow the Gospels' we have to say. But is not that

question begging? People are right to ask. For the case we are making hinges on interested witnesses — a situation which no ingenuity can circumvent. For other witnesses there are none. To have Jesus in any measure without them we lack not only the story but the teaching also. Hence the necessary effort of those who deplore the faith about him to discern, against it, the portraiture it dominates. This makes for an odd situation in that the sources have to be trusted to a degree in order to be corrected to a satisfaction. The vicissitudes of Gospel formation have to be probed in order, if possible, to sift the wheat from the chaff by the winnowing wisdom of the scholars. It is a praiseworthy enterprise now bewilderingly complicated and often irresolute and conjecture-prone.

The intelligent Christian learns to live with this situation. That it cannot be eluded is part of the honesty of faith, not to say the energy of truth. But we have to realise how fraught it is, and cannot fail to be, with prejudices which stem back into theology. The community actually possessing him has somehow, on this showing, to be neutralised to admit of our possessing him. Contemporaries, then, have to be both heeded and queried for contemporaries now. Jesus has to be 'recovered' from his own legatees whom we can only trust distrustfully. Any Muslim would think that crucial documents ought to be more absolute, more categorical. And Jews must think themselves better served with an oral Law that contains all that original Sinai was meant to give.

The Christian's New Testament, for good or ill, is not that way. We cannot take it painlessly 'at face value,' yet it is our crucial interface with Jesus Christ. The situation involves the learned in many devices. Hints or tokens of a Jesus different from the Christ of faith which can be detected as surviving anyhow within a record which might be assumed to have suppressed them, are deemed to be the more significant. Similarly, emphases which bear the stamp of later faith must be suspect because they were superimposed upon a different original. Thus a critic's prejudice tends to determine his analyses. A Jesus who comments: 'Why do you call me good? none is good but God . . .' is authentic because the evangelist must be expected to have excluded such a comment. That it persists tells us how strong and rooted the tradition was, to have been thus retained. Contrary-wise, a Jesus who says, even in the Synoptic Gospels: 'No man knows the Father but the Son' must, in such language, be overlaid with the inauthentic. Or it is obviously right to hear Jesus limit his mission to 'the lost sheep of the house of Israel' — a sentiment a world-wide Church must have deplored but, even so, did not eliminate. However, a Jesus who talks of a 'gospel preached throughout the whole world' must be the gloss of later 'Gentile' ardour and not the dependable theme in Galilee, cosmopolitan as Galilee certainly was.

In such ways 'did Jesus intend the Church?' receives answers which vary with assessments reached beyond the particular texts which trouble or confirm them. What is open to faith is not foreclosed to question. Consensus may be partial where conviction is complete. The mythologiser reads the same Scriptures as the Christian. All of which goes to underline how faith has the nature of decision, but it is not a decision that is blind or casual.

There is one area of the New Testament story where this 'hide and seek' situation for scholarship is especially germane to verdicts about the intention of Jesus and the decision of the Church and how these relate together. It concerns the record of the last evening and the Last Supper. What did Jesus 'institute'? How did it belong with his purpose? Have the texts told it rightly? Does it warrant the doctrinal meaning which both faith and sacrament presently gave to it in theology and liturgy?

'The bread which we break' as 'a partaking of the body of Christ' in Christian devotion we noted briefly in chapter 4. But could there have been other meanings? The sense of impending crisis lies heavily over all. Did it have to do with the agony of redemptive love? Or was it the tension of peril on the eve of a bid for insurrectionary power or a precipitation of Messianic drama from heaven? Or was it groping foreboding at the sense of a mission now trapped and forlorn? How did he, how did they, read the invocation of Passover parallels? What Exodus was the morrow to bring — from futility, or hiddenness, or powerlessness, or from none of these, but rather exodus into the achievement of a world's redemption? What were, in the light of Jesus' story, the anticipations of the Cross?

Interpreters who trust the story will answer with the Church: those who do not trust it will, precisely by their distrust, make the antecedent story different. Such is the choice of faith. To ask what, or which, is the more credible is to be thrown back on to the criteria by which we judge. The faith may be mistaken but is there any faith worthy of the name which may not be?

This issue of Holy Communion or Messianic enigma impinges strongly on another theme of faith's interrogation. 'I will not drink again with you until I drink it newly in My Father's Kingdom,' he said. Is this another of those sayings which might have been suppressed and yet survived to be embarrassing? How does it tally with 'He was known of them in the breaking of the bread.'? What 'kingdom' did he await? Is the reference to the Messianic banquet and was this thought to supervene very rapidly on the morrow of his dying? What, continuing the question, of the *Parousia,* or 'appearing' of Jesus again which undoubtedly the first Church had in immediate prospect? Resurrection appearances did not fulfill this expectation. For they were private and intimate. When they ceased the Church waited. Are we to say because no *Parousia* transpired that he and they were mistaken and faith, therefore, discredited?

The impressive fact here is the way in which the heart of the Messianic faith outlived the non-appearing of the returning Lord. Far from annulling the decisive conviction a delayed, even abandoned, *Parousia* came to be read as a long-range dimension of hope. 'He that had come' was 'He that is to be' in the meaning of 'He that is.' There is a deep resemblance here to a strain in current Judaism with one radical difference.

For many in Jewry, down the centuries and notably of late, the Messianic, never yet dependably identified in event, has become pure futurism. To believe in 'Messiah' is to live hopefully in a world that remains 'unredeemed.' 'Messiah' can never play his hand: any supposed actuality must mean the foregoing of any Messianism beyond it. In order never to be postdated by evil, Messiah' must always be 'not yet.'

Jewish thinkers, and some secular ones, have held this against
the Christian identification of authentic Messiahship in Jesus,
citing both the continuity of evil beyond the alleged point
of our redemption *and* the failure of any *Parousia* which the
first Christians anticipated as the vindication of the Messiah
they had identified. It is clear in the New Testament that,
alongside the earliest immediacy of hope, runs a sense of
long vistas and receding horizons, a faith that the future has
to be entrusted, in its hiddenness, to the love and sovereignty which *have* been disclosed. There is both Messianic
actuality and Messianic hope, the one undergirding and
qualifying the other.

Such Christian futurism survived the lapse of first and
immediate hope because it saw the present task of the
Messianic community in the light of Jesus' Messianic
reality. Non-*Parousia* did not extinguish that actuality. The
significance of the Cross, as love's active bearing of the wrong,
endured. 'In him,' they said, 'we have our redemption through
his blood.' They could recall in Eucharist 'the body and the
blood,' not as a martyrdom denied its celestial climax,
but as the price of a grace which had, indeed, redeemed them
and required them to become redeemers 'in the kingdom
and patience of Jesus Christ.' They did not have to deny to
themselves any past faith in order to hold a future hope. They
had the latter in the meaning of the former. Unfolding
time-scales did not deprive them of the one or the other.
That the Church survived the non-*Parousia*, far from being
the disproving of its faith, constitutes a clear evidence of its
resilience. It demonstrates in what that faith essentially
consisted. The wounds of Jesus as index to the love of God
were not about a calendar of hope but the very time of grace.
Even so, it was a decision of faith which saw it so. Those who
find the lack of *Parousia* the faith's undoing reckon without
the future that did happen in the faith's ongoing, within the
New Testament itself.

In sum, one may fairly conclude that in presenting its
Christ to the Graeco-Roman world the New Testament
dependably preserves the Jewishness of its Jesus. When
'Hellenising' in Christology is wisely assessed it leaves no
case for a 'reJudaising' of Jesus. His Jewishness is mediated

within his discovered relevance to all. So to conclude is an intelligent decision of faith, seeing that the very data on which we have to conclude are data from faith. It is open, however, to reach a contrary conclusion. Faith does not stand in the suppression of its critics. Nor does it offer guarantees that are indisputable. Its inward fibre is decision, its outward posture is commendation. Our retrospect reinforces our original conviction, namely that Christianity derives from Christ via Christians, These are not absolutists: they are witnesses, and the first of them were witnesses by sight and hand and, only so, by word and pen.

In highlighting this crucial factor of decision there are two final questions we must undertake. The one is the view that makes 'decision' all there was, detaching it from any reliable nexus with a history. The other is the denial that there was any decision at all.

A school of New Testament criticism has arisen this last half century which sees the Christ-faith of the Church as itself the 'event' of the Gospel and the only 'event' there was. It is a school of thought with two broad sources, the one is an oddly pessimistic view as to what we can really know of Jesus, the other is the impact of philosophies of existentialism.

For these thinkers the Gospels can yield us little or no dependable account of the actual Jesus. 'The quest of the historical Jesus' — to use the familiar phrase of Albert Schweitzer — defeats itself, the data being irretrievably obscure, contradictory and inconclusive. The evangelists are hopelessly 'interested' parties. They can afford us no sure, critical, authentic guidance in determining who, how, even whether, Jesus really was. Schweitzer's own conclusions, he felt, would torpedo once and for all the traditional or orthodox confidence about him and scatter the futilities of Christian piety in the harsh, bleak wind of contradiction. Others, too, who differ sharply from Schweitzer's own characterisation of Jesus, share his disavowal of New Testa-ment credentials and 'church-faith.'

Whether disconcerting to popular beliefs, or simply sceptical and negative, such wide distrust of the Gospels may be said, in a strange sort of way, not to matter. What matters, for example to Rudolf Bultmann, a scholar with whose name this stance is strongly linked, is the will of the disciples to believe. The fact of faith rather than the facts of history determines Christianity. The real event was the preaching, apart from the historicity of its theme. *Kerugma* — the Greek term for preaching, or the thing heralded — may turn on 'myth' but is not thereby disqualified. On the contrary, there can never be any other ground for faith than faith itself. That the apostles believed Jesus to be the dying, risen Saviour, the Christ of God, suffices. Believing — with this intensity and range — makes it so. If, then, we are asking how to derive 'Christianity', we must conclude that we can derive it only from 'Christians'. The 'Christ' was an identity for whom they alone were responsible, whom they alone sustained. In a sense faith requires no proving, since its proof is in itself.

It needs no great acumen to see how this assessment fits the stance of the existentialists, or rather those of them so minded. For life is not speculation, it is commitment. In ethics, in conduct, in society, in personal awareness, we are confronted all the time with the need to decide, to act. Time itself does not admit of suspension of decision. For it will make even our indecision decisive by its own thrust and sequence. We cannot elude the need to opt, to live, to choose. Being in the world we must be at the world. Abeyance of will is the will overridden. Time will not wait.

Such perpetual challenge to the will must hustle any mere interrogation of, or from, the mind. The latter is merely an instrument, an informant, of the will. Religion is no exception. Indeed it is the cardinal area of this experience of the necessity to be rather than to cogitate. Accordingly, for Christian existentialists, we find ourselves confronted by 'Christ' for decision. Embodying the supreme claim upon our loyalty, he challenges us to decide. He represents for us the focal point on which the will turns. The Church itself began in an allegiance which was the clue to existence. Perennially the Gospel spells the same demand, not for historical research but for historic commitment — historic because the very meaning of our own existence.

Jesus, then, is 'mythical', not in the common sense of 'legendary' and non-factual (unless we want to think so evidentially), but in the subtle sense that he represents a meaning, becomes the symbolic point of an experience. *Kerugma* and 'myth' are, in this way, inter-acting: the one offers what the other enshrines. And 'myth' in this sense neither needs nor suits mere historical, archaeological, critical, investigation, because it functions in the will. The will is moved by imagination and imagination can be independent of the findings of historians. So, however pessimistic we may feel we have to be about who, how and whether Jesus was, we can dispense with such anxieties. We need not deplore what research has not resolved. Faith is not thereby weakened. Nor would it be better warranted if we could be better satisfied on those counts of history we must, and do, transcend.

All the foregoing chapters will have made it clear that it was not decision in these terms we had in view. In setting 'Christian' as the middle term between 'Christ' and 'Christianity' we were in no sense eliding the first term. Nor did the vital role of Christians mean for us that their convictions were all there was of 'Christ.' We have not conceded 'myth' in the subtle sense by allowing it in the common sense. That symbol has its role and imagination its hold belongs with the distinction we earlier made between fact and truth. To that extent mythologisers have a point. But to dissociate the undoubted event of the *kerugma* from Jesus as 'event' is to be either in defiance or in despair of history. Neither defiance nor despair are legitimate.

It is fair to enquire why a purely existential *kerugma* should have bothered to write gospels or why a faith, supposedly enveloped in the providence of God, should have been saddled with the problematics — as we have acknowledged them to be — of written texts. That situation is surely for the humility, the honesty, the integrity of faith. A *kerugma*, properly understood, cannot well originate itself. Nor is good news self-generating. What Christians preached has to be one with Jesus 'in the flesh.' The tensions of Scripture must be reinstated. For the evasion of them, however subtly argued, is unworthy of a kerugmatic confidence. By the same token, we must be alert — as we saw in chapter 3 — to the way in which the experience of the preaching Church con-

ditioned the portrayal of the preached Christ. But those very
problematics which lead some mythologisers to near despair
about Jesus' history, only arise (and can only be undertaken)
in awareness of their living context. To that extent the
existentialists are not existentialist enough. They use their
theory to absolve themselves of its obligations. To believe in
the faith that launched the Church is to be the more urgently
involved with the Jesus who launched the faith. To be ready
to abandon sight of such a Jesus (however strenuous and
furtive the glimpses may be thought to be) is surely to render
one's faith the less responsive, the more enigmatic, the less
from him, the more from ourselves. Will that be its due and
real commendation? It will hardly be a faith reconcilable
with either the text or the temper of the New Testament.
Decision there certainly was, and must continue to be, but
it was not, and cannot well now be, detached from the onus
of its own first documentation. Nor need we be in any radical
despair. Those documents, Gospels and Epistles, may be still
the underwriters of our faith.

There remains the contrasted case which insists that there
was never any decision at all. Christianity has never been
one thing. There was no original Christian faith. Nor has
there been any decisive statement of Christian faith that holds
a norm for all time. What the other theorists dub the 'myth'
of an Incarnate Lord, these describe as the 'myth' of
Christian beginnings. The apostolic Church, on this view,
is woefully idealised. There were tensions and contradictions
from the start. We hear only from the victorious party with
no adequate hearing for those, shall we say, the strongly
Judaic Christians, who lost out in the steady 'Gentilising' of
the faith. Lacking the presumed minority verdicts, we
cannot be sure of the majority.

Moreover, so this case runs, all cultures need their sacred
memories and these, to serve their purposes, must be
ideally hallowed. The New Testament, accordingly, depicts
a much greater unity than in fact existed and contrives to
obscure what might tell against its cherished vision. Readers
must perforce be sceptical about any unitary past. Furthermore, authentic Christians must be forward looking. 'Time
makes ancient good uncouth.' Apostolicity is not our

proper talisman. We have to discriminate for ourselves within the endless diversity of what 'Christianity' has since become and of how elusive was, and is, the Messianic theme. Even Constantine, the antithesis of New Testament powerlessness, and seeing the Cross as the banner to adorn his armies, could be hailed as a 'Messiah.' The vagaries of Christendom have effectively denied identity to Christianity. What decided Christianity becomes, therefore, a deluded study, an exercise in futility.

Some aspects here will be proper to chapter 7 to follow. But all in all, it is an odd case. Consensus may never be complete and was not so among the apostles. But there is no identifying where it fails or falters without some discernible reality. To think of Christianity as being whatever Christians, through two millenia, have said it is, is only to engage with whatever warranted the name they carry. That of which there is nothing definite has no identity. If it cannot be characterised it cannot be assessed. Idealising there may well have been, though there is much honest realism within the New Testament. There are, indeed, many loose ends in the Acts of the Apostles. 'Orthodoxy,' in any sphere, tends to be tentative and proximate before it is so named. Intelligent New Testament study leaves room for tender consciences and open ends. But the idea, and the fact, of a canonised Scripture, albeit generated by spontaneous action, serve — as they also pre-suppose — a faith that exists by decision, a faith which believes it has a substance which it is careful to delimit and conserve, dynamic as its nature is.

Ongoing development and the transformation which time brings necessarily proceed within an identity which can be held to have undergone them. Where change is alleged to have been total we are left denying anything in which it has occurred. To say that nothing was ever definitively Christian is to evacuate the term. Its founding identity was both the making and the theme of the New Testament. 'Today,' in the language of Hebrews 13.8, turns upon that 'yesterday,' the 'yesterday' and the 'today' of the 'same Jesus,' whom the writer there invites his readers to keep ardently in their thoughts. He links that Jesus firmly with leaders and mentors of the faith-community for whom the abiding Jesus was the goal of existence, the issue of their lives and the seal of their careers. He finds, that is, in the steadfast proving of Christians the unfailing proof of the Christ. It is just this mutuality we have been at pains throughout to understand.

There will always be an uneasy relationship between the historian and the believer, the pursuit of fact and the embrace of truth. It is readily possible to relate to Jesus, as students, historians, even as archaeologists, wholly in terms of unanswered questions. It has often been done. We may well honour the will to integrity behind the insistent misgivings about verdicts that reach any certainty. Yet 'the Jesus of unanswered questions', notwithstanding, is already answered — and the questions with him — in the verdict of response. Those *about* him we must hold within the question *from* him. 'What think ye of the Christ?' was not a query for pundits or debaters, but disciples. Coming from the questioner-Jesus, it turns the tables on the merely captious. He is not duly 'thought on' in the detachment, the observer-stance, the indecision, into which mere interrogatives may beguile us. For the apparent openness of questions may well conceal a bias in which the very pursuit of 'truth' may neutralise its presence. Beyond the inquisition of fact is the comprehension of love. Such love, given and received, lives with interrogatives and does not impatiently suppress them. The minds that then interpret move within the motives that surrender. The final integrity is the consent of love. The onus on us passes from inconclusive scrutiny to open-ended faith.

So it was with the generations within the New Testament. So it has always been. Is such Christianity still transactable? What of the perennial decision now?

CHAPTER 7

The Perennial Decision Now

The Greek and New Testament word for truth, *aletheia*, whatever its derivation, has an intriguing hint in its making. For Lethe, in the Greek mysteries, was the daughter of Eris and personified oblivion. She gave her name to the water from which the dead drank as they passed into utter forgetfulness. The particle *a* has to do with being contrary, as in 'agnostic', one who disclaims *gnosis* or knowledge. *Aletheia*, then, may be understood as the repudiation of unawareness, a set of mind and spirit open to meaning, alert to reality and sensitive. 'Truth', in human experience, has to abjure the casual and the inattentive. Whatever the cloisters of its discipline there can be no cloisters for its mind. It intends and requires an honesty that seeks no exemption from disquiet, no soporific of the soul. The waters of its baptism do not convey us into dreamlike abeyance of the will to be.

Having reviewed what was decisive in original Christianity it is well to set ourselves the state of mind that *aletheia* exacts of all her seekers and her lovers in a will to be — and stay — awake. To be 'at ease in Zion' is no merely ancient habit: many have been 'lulled in Christendom'. There is a temper in tradition tending to complacence, with more than a hint of 'Do not disturb' upon the door.

Admittedly, a state of being sanguine about faith and discipleship is, doubtless, less prone to happen in the climate of our time, when to be 'ill at ease' in church, or at least about it, is the likelier condition of the soul. This is precisely what Paul's language implies in the key passage about the 'constraining love of Christ'. For his verb, as we saw, has to do with what has to make its way strongly against what impedes it, as the woman did who 'touched the hem of Jesus' garment' despite the throng and press around him. One in a crowd with an aim in view like hers has to contend with the weight against the will, the thrust that wills otherwise — if it wills at all — from the medley around. The mass has its own momentum whether or not it knows its own mind and what is private has to compete with what is public. The constraint of urgent faith meets — and must surmount — the restraints of randomness around.

No strange metaphor, this in Paul, for the currrent pressures upon faith. 'The love of Christ constrains,' we might say, against the grain of what prevails around us with its own purposes or aimlessness. The image of the person in the crowd, of the self in the scene, fairly captures the tests and toughness of belief and belonging, of the soul's reach towards the Christ. There is that in our context which would make us desist, would turn our resolve into reluctance and have us capitulate to indifference or surrender to anonymous living, drifting with the human tide. We only know the love and the constraining in letting them control. Such is their *aletheia.*

There is something of this situation in another crucial saying of Paul, when he writes to Christians at Rome: 'I am not ashamed of the Gospel of Christ . . .' (Romans 1.16) Why should he be? we might ask. Does he not write elsewhere about glorying in that Gospel? Why should he think it necessary to disclaim any shame? Why the strange denial? If we conclude that the reason lies in the 'scandal' of the Gospel, its being about a criminal's death, about a cross and thorns and seeming felony, then his protest becomes a counter thrust, a repudiation of revulsion, a saluting of the scandalous. His not being ashamed is a conscious rebuttal of the implication that he ought to be. He has caught the mood of resistance and is alerted to reply. What he writes in Romans is one with what he tells the Corinthians. He knows what the 'constraining' is because like 'Jerusalem compassed with armies' (which his metaphor suggests) he is aware of what presses in the opposite direction. Just as momentum overcomes inertia so his conviction masters whatever deters it in the mind and spirit.

The day of those first Christians stands in such sharp contrast to ours. The pressures now are not the pressures

then. How should we characterise what 'the constraining love
of Christ' encounters in our time? What of the jostle of ideas,
the press of perplexity, through which, against which, it must
now make its way with us and in us? The will to faith has
long frontiers with the will to doubt. What constrains us to
be Christian has many reconnoitres with the will to be
otherwise in the lively mind.

'Looking over a very wide field,' as John Bunyan's Evangelist
required of his Pilgrim-Christian, we consider four features
of the contemporary situation where the faith we have
studied in the New Testament is most strenuously at issue.
These will be far from exhausting the themes that engage
the disciple and the sceptic. They will do full justice to
neither. But they will measure in some sense what a constraining to decision means for the former precisely by counsel
with the latter. In taking stock of the disincentives to belief
we can hope to 'develop' from those 'negatives' — as photo-
graphers say — a clearer image of the things believed. For,
given the character of decision which we have stressed
throughout, faith cannot but be tempered, if not refined,
by converse with the indecisive and the honest company of
the unpersuaded. We can best review all the ground we have
covered by traversing it again in the mind-set of other
options about our human-ness, its mystery, its wounds and
its destiny.

Perhaps it will be agreed that the first decisive faith
constituting Christianity runs counter, in this our day, to
attitudes we must assess in four areas. Realism about its
history finds it wanting. Political realism with the themes of
power holds it flawed and faulted. It is at odds with the
instincts of contemporary thinking. Finally it goes against
the grain of a personal realism about our experience of finite,
mortal being in a self. On all these points, as we anticipated
in the Introduction, it is held historically unconvincing,
politically delinquent, conceptually outdated and personally
illusory. On these several counts it is seen as disproven in
its own story, effete in its idealism, archaic in its concepts
and, in its urge for consolation, a crutch for cripples.

If these items do not succeed in being comprehensive at
least they will not be held to fail in candour. We measure

the constraint *to* faith by wrestling with what constrains *against* it. The frankness is appropriate to both. Those interior questions involving chapter 6 will be latent in these wider, sharper issues. The tasks which are domestic to faith are properly to be distinguished from those that attend its external relations.

History's grim indictment of Christianity is too vast and varied for rehearsal here. Cynics as well as penitents have long ruminated on the tangle of iniquity incriminating institutional faith and hierarchy. Must it be assumed that the incipient faith was only safe in the catacombs? What if only beginnings can be wholesome? if pristine faith has no staying power in the real world? How does it happen that the very Cross itself, the clue to the love that must constrain becomes, in the pride and passion of its heralds, the goad to war and hatred? How does the universalism which broke through the stubborn otherness of Jew and Gentile, embracing both in equal grace, betray itself in surrender to the most virulent nationalisms and activate malevolent rejection of the Jew? Can it clear itself of the Judaic suspicion that its univeralism is altogether phoney, a false pretence of human community sustaining aggressive national monopolies of the divine favour? Is it not altogether plain that Christian Messianism was, and is, at best premature and at worst illusory? It is not merely that we have been celebrating Easter too soon, but that we ourselves are the grimmest proof of it. If Jesus' tomb was ever empty, must the sceptic say, have not his alleged people re-interred him and finally sealed the stone? Is not the Gospel quite discredited in the folly, the pride, the malice, the stridency, of the company it keeps?

It will not suffice to observe that all religions, in the stress of their temptations, connive with their own disproof, conspire to their own undoing. Comparison of religions would be odious indeed, in this regard. But none has so precious, so vulnerable, a heritage in trust as Christianity. None is so liable to reproach from its own origin against its further story. For none proposes so blessedly about God, none so ambitiously about mankind. Faiths with a more modest agenda of salvation might escape so dire rebuke.

The capacity for self-condemnation may often have been

tragically wanting in historic Christianity: the criteria never
were. For they were present in the very content of the first
decision. What matters about any faith is their frame of
reference about themselves, what judges them from within.
External reckonings and indictments may well be valid and
urgent and are not to be evaded because they originate from
outside. Yet penitence about them has to be inwardly attained.
What makes faiths what they are has, in the end, to be the
source of what judges them. Otherwise the warrant of
inward authority will be liable to refuse the accusation.
Religions are adept at their own exoneration.

Is there a surer capacity for self-reproach about its
custodians than that implicit in the faith of 'Christ crucified'
as 'the power and the wisdom of God'? Christian sequels
betray, but can never escape, the Christian origins. Disloyalties
and treacheries emerge, dominate and deprave across the
centuries. But they only do so in defiance of the great original
which has already given them the lie. The principle at the
heart of Jesus' Messiahship avails in any and every encounter
with evil, no less with treasons inward than with wrongs
without. The Cross has often most to do with its own
community in trust.

For the Church to have been educated by the Cross and
the Resurrection of Jesus into the truth of grace, and to have
been inaugurated by the realisation, was, in itself, no
guarantee that it would keep faith with the meaning. It had
'the treasure in earthen vessels,' in the frailty of its own
liability to all the wiles of evil which attended its genesis in
the sufferings of Jesus. For those sufferings were index both
to what wrong demands for its saving and to what alone
suffices the saving. All Christian sins and failures, as history
indicts them, return us to the risks and realism of a grace
authentic only in the keeping of those who will to bear its
image and to live by its life.

To know it so is no plea of exoneration. On the contrary,
it is to recognise that there is no immunity from the secret
of the Cross in the trust of telling it. It was the lengthening
of the trust in the accumulation of corporate tradition and
its adoption by the interests of custodians generated in its
name, which made for the compromises and then the guilt

manifested, so long and so far, in the flux of centuries. These
have frequently issued into negations of the Gospel itself,
negations so complete that they have been surreptitiously
presented as affirming it.

Sceptics will urge that, in this light, the source, too, is
discredited, being so evidently unable to ensure its own
continuity or surmount the corrupting and the deploring
for ever dogging its story in the world. Is not the praise of
its alleged origin quite extinguished in the reproach of its
actual record? That the conflict has been perennial none
can deny. Yet the fact remains that the heart of the Gospel
has been the most radical ground of quarrel with the record.
The Gospel being what it is, the trust of it carries the criterion
of judgement more tellingly than any other source of
accusation and — indeed — more hopefully. For that the
faith of Jesus and the faith about him should be so
precariously entrusted, so hardly served, in the world is
only the other side of the grace which it tells, a grace which
risks and gives all into our human fallenness and which
chooses to succeed with us and through us only in the
freedom of its own patience and compassion. Those who
see it all as, unhappily, a fond and futile idealism, have not
reckoned with a realism so long-suffering or thought it could
be divine.

A major factor in 'the grieving of the Spirit' (cf. Ephesians
4.30) belongs in the tangle of faith and politics. In its first
definition *via* Messiah Jesus and *via* the decisive Christian
perception of him, Christianity was innocent both of
nationality and statehood. In the celebrated words of the 2nd
century Epistle to Diognetus, Christians believed themselves
aliens in every country and yet everywhere at home. Such
was for them the meaning of 'the kingdom of heaven' and
community 'in Christ'. That quality of decision has profound
significance for ourselves today. The implications of its sense
of an allegiance astride all ethnic borders and beyond all
political confinement witnesses to the contemporary need
to relativise the identities which diversify humanity into
tribes, states, cultures and power-systems. These are to be seen
as indeed within a doctrine of creation and have their due,
but relative, role in collective society. But their trend has been

always to competition, confrontation, enmity and absolute demand. It was both a right acknowledgement and necessary subjection of these which Christian decision in its New Testament shape assumed and enjoined.

It did so by a firm openness to 'whosoever willed' to enter within it on the ground of faith and by a complete innocence of the power equation. Some would say that the latter was purely circumstantial. The faith arose in the context of the Roman Empire and, as measured by suffering, in spite of it. It did, and could, have no pretension to political power. But such innocence of power, far from being mere circumstance, derived directly from the pattern of Jesus as Messiah. This insistence of early Christianity on 'faith alone' as the condition of belonging *and* as the way within the world, is however, found quite wanting by, for example, the tradi-tional logic of Islam. For Muslims religion without state-power is lax, at risk, fragile, and inept. In Muhammad's reading of destiny there had to be the Hijrah or emigration from the Mecca of pure preaching to the Medina of power-consolidation. The Prophet had to become the prophet-armed, the teacher the inducer — by the legitimate exercise of battle and control.

So moulded at its origin, classical Islam has always believed in the religious validity of the state. Modern Zionism, in its own different idiom, makes the same equation between faith, identity, and the possession of power. Within such establishments others of different faith may subsist pro-vided they submit politically. Occupancy of territory, in political rule, is in some form, also assumed to be vital not merely to survival but to identity itself.

In that sense modern Zionism represents a deep — and not unanimous — decision within the soul of Jewry that, without state-territory control, religion itself is for ever at risk. So deciding, Zionism rejected a long and honoured counter-tradition in Jewry which, in some respects, resembled closely that assumed by the first Christian churches, namely dispersion in any territory, under any sovereignty, as those whose being was sufficiently defined and authen-tically expressed in spiritual identity inwardly assured if outwardly at risk.

To the 'realism' which insists on the indispensable role of political sovereignty in the securing of religion, later Christian history has paid long and costly tribute. It did not make a Hijrah out of catacombs into thrones. The Empire under Constantine finally abandoned persecution and took over the Church. When, through successive centuries of its 'Holy Roman' existence, Christianity cherished and wielded the political order, the pristine pattern was wholly forfeited, so far so that 'Christ' and imperialism were taken to be synonymous. In modern history in Europe nation-states made their versions of Christian faith the warrant and captive of their power, a captivity often held in utmost pleasure in the warrant. The story is long, tangled and beset with confusion and controversy. Our purpose with it here is only to recover — from beyond it in the past it overlaid — the immediate, contemporary meaning of what it betrayed or misconceived, namely a faith which gladly, instinctively, subsisted in a dispersion it saw as its natural condition and in an innocence of power-sanction which it derived from its Messiah in Jesus. It transcended the ethnic and the territorial in breaking open the most tenacious divide, that between Jew and Gentile. It had no lust of power despite the traumas through which it passed and despite the kindling legacy of the Maccabees and the upsurge of their ardour in the Jewish Revolt running in parallel with Christian evangelism.

Given how far the Christian centuries have been implicated in repudiation of their origins, and given the present-day search for human community transcending the near-obsolescence of traditional nationalisms, and given the tensions in the situation of divergent religious faiths, it is urgent to set clearly in focus this double content of original Christianity, namely its any-place, any-people quality and its non-power, non-hegemony instinct, and urgent, also, to see how both were grounded in the Christ as 'Christians' decided for him and about him and, in the deciding, were themselves defined. The case we made earlier sustains us now.

The original Christian reading of human evil turned on the fact that a deep expression of it was there at the very heart of faith's own story. There could be no ignoring the mystery of wrong for those whose faith stemmed from the

Cross. Nor, given such a dark and desperate experience, could
they have stayed with theory and abstract philosophy aloof
from grief and wounds. When the Gospel wrote of that event
as 'the sin of the world' ('sin' in the singular), it did not forget
that crucifixions could happen daily by the score, yearly by
the thousand. It knew well enough that no single execution
could exclusify evil. The world was too old, too wide, too
callous, for that. But it did believe that one event, in its
significance, could inclusify evil, could represent in its
motivation and its logic, what is wrong with our humanity.
'All mankind's epitome' might be enshrined in a single deed
in the light of which we might realise, for all time, what is
'the iniquity of us all.' The Christianity of the Gospels
understood the Cross as the index to the perversity to which
human collectives are prone. Pleas about 'place and nation'
had played their part. Impulses, political, social, religious,
in the tangle of personal motives, had been responsible. The
ironical 'Ecce homo' of Pilate captured a drama, an assembly,
a trial, an encounter, yet more aptly entitled: 'Ecce homines,'
'behold us humans.'

An awareness of 'the sin of the world,' of that order, must
necessarily have had long thoughts about the power dimension in the human scene and its several organs of state, race,
empire and territory. But not only so: at the heart of the same
event, in the pattern of the central figure, lay an index to
what wrong demands for its saving and what, alone, suffices
to save. In the wake of resurrection the Church knew 'the
Lamb of God who bears the sin of the world.' Coming so
to know is, in part, what resurrection meant. Being educated
into the truth of things by the twin lessons of the Cross as
to evil and its saving, the Church in its genesis had in trust
the clue to its own postures in the world vis-à-vis 'the
principalities and powers', as Paul called them, the structures
and citadels of power, as we would call them now.

The meaning of that education was that religion, at least
as expressed in Christianity, had tasks *with* the powers of this
world, and also tasks *against* them, and — supremely —
tasks *beyond* them. By this logic, faith could never be unilaterally identified with any racial particular nor be part
and parcel of any political régime. By some religious lights

of long assurance and persistence in history it was, and is, a logic to be rejected as unrealistic on every count. Much in the story of Christianity down the centuries has endorsed that rejection. But there is no mistaking the verdict and decision of the New Testament. There certainly are tasks *with* the powers. That 'they do not bear the sword in vain,' (Romans 13.4) in no way means that they always bear it justly, wisely or soundly. The imagery of the Book of Revelation bears witness to that. But the political order is indispensable to social existence. The role of the Christian community is to recognise and serve that order in a critical awareness of its vocation to the common good. But a Christian realism knows that it will only be a modicum of justice, wellbeing and integrity that the political order can attain and maintain.

That modicum is significant and urgent, to be enlarged and ensured as ideally as possible. This is the task *with* it to which the Christian as citizen and the community as church are committed, by the quality of their mind and conduct, to the utmost that occasion allows. Such, broadly, was the counsel and the achievement of pastoral concern in the New Testament Epistles, despite the suspicious oppressiveness of the Roman state. It was the task *against* the political order which aroused those suspicions, in respect of a more ultimate allegiance sealed in private ritual and incompatible with the deification of the Emperor and the absolute sovereignty of the state.

But it was the tasks *beyond* the political order which the apparent powerlessness of the Cross and the inaugural Christian 'innocence' of power underline most decisively. The modicum of public righteousness attainable by the political order, assuming it to be attained, leaves whole reaches of evil untouched and unretrieved, often even unidentified. What is, in the end, coercive may be necessary, even beneficial, but still, at best, only holding the ring for other factors. Laws and penalties, power-dimensions, may help stay the course of evil. But all coercion tends to enmity in that, in whatever name it is exercised, it restrains a will which is not transformed by the restraint. Penitence and forgiveness may ensue from restraints and penalties but are not generated by them. There is always that beyond the punitive or the accusatory which is needed if there is to be healing and reconciliation. For these there is always a price to be paid. There has to be a 'bearing' of the wrong beyond the retributive, beyond the coercive, and beyond the vindictive. For though these may shape some external corrective, they do not restore or redeem. By their very shape and temper they leave remainders of evil within both the situation and the soul which they have neither means nor imagination to resolve.

The Cross of Jesus at the heart of Christian decision was eloquent of the grievous travesties of which power is capable, but blessedly eloquent also of that 'bearing' by which alone wrong is overcome. In every evil situation there is a cost that love must undergo. Those who are 'overcome by evil,' whether in apathy, hatred, retaliation, or despair, forfeit the readiness to 'overcome by good.' So doing, they may elude the private consequences but only by retaining in the situation the entail of those attitudes. Only the costly outgoing of the will to the positive overcoming is the defeatist, acquiescent or malevolent 'being overcome' halted and reversed. It was such redeemers in society that the Cross of Jesus, as understood in Christian calling, exemplified and recruited. They were redeemers who became such by conforming to the significance, the logic, of Jesus' Messiahship.

It is this radical redemptiveness in society which answers the charge that the very powerlessness of the first Christians, their resolute non-politicising of their faith, despite insistent precedents to the contrary, were unfitted for the real world. On the contrary, says their original faith, the 'realism' which marries religion with tribe, nation, race, culture and statehood, is not realist enough. It may acquire sinews and sanctions which conduce to what the Qur'ān calls 'manifest victory.' It may find the political dominance, the active sovereignty which Muhammad exemplified and Islam took into instinctive partnership, but — so doing — it will forfeit its capacity to be at issue with itself about race and power. It will also impair its witness to the sovereignty of God in the very fact of identifying that sovereignty so closely with its own. Or it may accommodate its sense of divine

sovereignty to the current interests of the political order it
has religiously espoused. Either way, it will cease to be truly
religious.

Ours is a time when religions must find the humility to
share the guidance of the world. If they are to do so, their
interpretation of the world must not be in fee to the
compulsive ways of politics. Can it be in doubt that the stance
at the heart of New Testament Christianity resolved this most
crucial factor at the heart of religion itself? Its commendation of faith consisted only in the quality of an open
hospitality to mankind beyond the privacies of race and
culture. It was innocent of the persuasives which belong with
force or rule — persuasives which, at best, compromise the
integrity of faith and, at worst, destroy it.

But ours is also a time in which faith must find the
language to engage the attention of the world. If, dis-
claiming and disowning sanctions of power and race,
Christans seek only to be heard, from conviction for
conviction, it is well they should be articulate. Our third
broad disquiet about our situation was how well and how
far faith spoke its meaning, how far contemporary Christians
'let their discretion be their tutor' — a discretion which
discerns the distance there too often is between the climate
of the time and the vocabulary of belief.

The issue here is not simply the dominance of technology
and the sense it imposes of 'man in command' and of a
divine 'absentee.' There is enough about technology to make
at least the perceptive humble, apprehensive and possibly
awed and grateful — all of these religious perceptions. The
distinction we made earlier between 'fact' and 'truth' goes
far to meet the obtuseness that sees language as only trading
in observable data and 'verifiable' phenomena of the senses
and the sciences. While thankful for the laboratory and
moving in the market-place, ordinary souls know that their
world is more than these. The secularity which merely buys
and sells, promotes and profits, counts its gains and preens
itself that they will trickle down elsewhere, betrays its own
contradiction once the soul awakes or music stirs and poetry
mourns or celebrates. We must trust the human to know
when philosophies sell experience short and policies prove

unaware of how deep it runs. We can depend on the
sacramental principle, securely grounded in the doctrine of
creation and the Incarnation and the Eucharist, to undertake the hallowing of our experience against all that degrades
the givens of existence. In all our anxieties faith is the
antithesis of despair and truth has more resources than our
advocacy.

Nevertheless, they are such as to turn on our
resourcefulness. If the crisis currently is not the content of
the faith but its communication, then it is urgent that a wise
'discretion' teach us. And language, whether of word, of
symbol or of ritual, is where we must respond. How intelligible where it most needs to be — for the outsider —
is the faith we offer? 'Theology' — at least among politicians
— tends to be a synonym for what is either vacuous or
irrelevant, subtleties for their own sake. Even those dis-
posed to 'feel after God' are often deterred or non-plussed
by the forms, of word or ritual, by which institutional faith
accosts them.

That there are pitfalls here is plain enough. There are
moods to understand as well as meanings to be understood.
Some find congenial a faith which intimates rather than
explains, and distrust what strives above all to be intelligible. Much of the complaint over the Alternative Service
Book overlooks, or disowns, the merits of its objectives, and
deplores its alleged forfeiture of the 'feel' and 'diction' of
what is venerable and revered. For such, religion should not
use the language of daily life. It should not think its
meanings held to a concern for what is readily intelligible,
faith prospering most where there is least light. Allusiveness
— even elusiveness — may be more fitting in the presence
of divine mystery.

Such instincts are not to be insensitively over-ridden. We
do not purvey 'a talkative religion — the faith with too much
to say.' The urge to unravel is not always proper and
traditions, whether of language or of form, certainly have
their place in the affections of belief. Yet, if our custody of
truth is to be more than inward, traditional and private, we
must be alert to the suspicion of the outsider — or the
sceptic — that our words and habits of mind are only

privately indulged and securely immune from the questions
of the world. What may be seemly, even 'epic,' from within
may well be seen as ponderous or pointless from without.
'The things of God for the people of God' is a sadly
ambiguous, as well as a sweetly authentic, saying in the
Liturgy, if — enclosing a fellowship — it also forecloses it.
It is by reaching outward that we can best intensify what is
inward.

Doing so, we realise how far from ready comprehension,
not to say acceptance, is the 'word-shape' of Christian
doctrine. Are we not in need of creative ventures of
paraphrase in expression of 'the things most surely believed.'? To a degree which should cause us disquiet as
Christians one has to be 'to the manner born' if one is to
comprehend. 'Tell me the old, old story' was a song loved
of those who knew it already. For others it may, or may not,
be dimly there as that which is certainly old, and quaintly
'a story,' and there is little mind for its rehearsal. Unless the
'insider' takes urgent stock of this situation faith will be
indulging in unworthy privacy. To take up a lively task of
paraphrase into society's shape of thought will be the surest
answer to the notion that where Christians live they talk a
foreign language.

Take, for example, the idiom of John 3.16, so long treasured
by evangelists as the very essence of the Gospel and the theme
of saving faith: 'God so loved the world that He gave His
only begotten Son that . . .' How do we 'translate' from his
vocabulary into today's? How would John say it were he
writing now? John Keats, the poet, thought he had found
in the medium of 'imagination' shaping souls in the world
of nature 'a grander system of salvation than the Christian
religion' which he defined as 'being redeemed by a certain
arbitrary interposition of God and taken to heaven.' And not
all misconceptions since have been as gentle or as earnest
as his.

What should we say of 'the Son' as 'given' and of 'love as
giving.'? 'Gift' we can readily accommodate, but how could
it obtain from God to man, from the infinite to the historical?
How, unless by an occasion of 'human-ness' in a context of
time, a context demanding, as well as learning, all that such

'giving' would entail if it was to be veritably 'given.'? What might 'only begotten' mean, archaic as the term now is and confusingly physical in connotation? What but that the 'giving' in the 'given' was inclusive, entire, definitive, not partial or ambiguous, not of a sort to be ever obsolete or forfeit, as from One liable to change of mind. In the 'only' we must read a 'one-ly,' a completeness, a finality, and in 'begotten' an author-ing, an authority, a moving from love into need, from sovereignty into compassion, even as the impulse of the shepherd activates the search or the genius of the musician must create the symphony. The meaning is that in our human time and place divine love has tran-scribed itself in terms that incorporate the whole crisis of the human world.

Nothing 'arbitrary' here: for in the Cross the malady and the remedy belong together. John, in the Gospel, could capture that (3.14-15) in the imagery of 'the serpent in the wilderness.' Obsolete for us now — except in the insignia of pharmacology — that story made a knowing of the hurt a condition of the healing. So it is still in the meaning of repentance and faith. The idiom changes but the truth persists. The one has to be 'gathered' from the other. Salvation comes only in the full measure of the tragedy. That is how it was in Jesus crucified. The 'lifting up', in John's discourse, might well be opaque, if not repulsive, its double meaning hidden, until we 'take its point' into proper reckoning.

So it is with all the rich analogy and metaphor of Christian meanings: 'the throne of . . . the Lamb,' the coming 'down from heaven,' the 'being crucified with Christ,' 'the perfect law of liberty,' and 'the fulness of the Godhead bodily.' With all these, and many more, the onus on the Christian now is to find equivalence of truth in freshness of thought, as part of loyalty itself. Confessions of faith may become no more than formulae if we cannot, or will not, state them anew in a language not traditionally theirs.

What is at issue here is not that misnomer, 'de-mythologization.' Nor is it 'reductionism.' 'Myth,' in the strict sense is simply storied metaphor and metaphor is what 'lets meaning mean' and 'truth tell' within the soul. To abjure it is to impoverish the mind itself. The resources of faith must undertake to turn the tables on those who find its themes and vocabulary suspect or vacuous by commending them in a translation that truly carries. Traditional language may then come back into its own but only because now charged with living comprehension and no longer secreted in a static form of words or imprisoned in inattentive dogma, unaware of its liabilities as perplexity must shape them.

But the task is formidable. A stance of bare authority may be more congenial and certainly less exacting. Such a stance will seem to some the only option of loyalty. Yet the faith has consciously and painfully to exist on behalf of those who do not now share it. Unless 'the people of God' are to be ingrown 'the things of God' must be outgoing. Only so will the inner *koinonia* between them be authentic. In the end the outside world's charge of obsolescence will be deserved short of our theology actively disproving it. That the faith of Christ is eminently translateable into all the puzzlements and distresses and aspirations of contemporary life is implicit in our holding it at all.

There is one aspect of this field for interpretation which can well lead from the third area of current challenge to our fourth, from the reproach of the incomprehensible to the suspect nature of personal consolation. What once 'decided Christianity' is now often out of court as being a fond illusion as well as a superseded account of human experience. The two sources of doubt or dismissal come together in the feature of Christian faith and devotion characteristic of so much hymnology and of the traditional Collects in the Prayer Book. These are so concerned, often also sentimentally, with personal needs, fears and anxieties and pre-occupations. Is faith no more than a will for the illusion of comfort, an improper quest for the sort of reassurance real life cannot allow us?

So much, at least, the Buddhist world would say and those minded to its mood. What first decided, and still finally decides, Christianity was, and is, on this view, excessively concerned with the point, and fate, of personality. Death concentrates the mind but, for Christians, does so too tenderly, too wistfully, too earnestly. They are so solicitous for eternal relevance and their part in it. And, whether it be in appraisal of death, or of life, it is personality — our own — which holds centre stage. Ought we not to call in question that centrality, and deny ourselves the illusion — as certainly others hold it to be — of a personal significance either here or 'there'? Can we register the sheer numbers of humanity and not allow that, as *dramatis personae* in our brief moment of mortality, we are negligible, ephemeral and eternally inconsequential? What decided Christianity must be seen in right perspective as pretentious, a conviction about significance in terms which cannot hold.

Critics from this angle, sounding brave and realist, find their evidence in our poems and our singing, and in the supplications of the Liturgy. That 'at the last we may come to His eternal joy,' breathes a quiet dignity but other language is more exuberant.

> 'Soon the night of weeping
> Shall be the morn of song . .'

sounds too romantic when 'scornful wonder' at 'the sore oppressed' is scarcely today's sentiment about the churches. The Prayer Book Collects in their yearning for 'security' here and hereafter doubtless echo the acute anxieties of the Tudor time, lest the land should lapse back into the conflict of 'the Wars of the Roses.' But something more adventurous would be proper now. Is it there in:

> 'Bid my anxious fears subside:
> Death of death, and hell's destruction,
> Land me safe on Canaan's side:
> Songs of praises I will ever give to Thee'?

'Fight the good fight,' may sound adventurous. But 'thou art dear, His arms are near,' sings the soul addressing itself. Is it only sounding heroic in a subtle quest for re-assurance? So the agnostic suspects, perhaps priding himself on a better realism about a bleaker world. Christians are liable to take themselves too seriously, too tenderly. They are too solicitous for themselves to look — even glance — into the void. They avert that gaze and romanticize.

'Earth's redeemer, plead for me,
Where the songs of all the sinless
Sweep across the crystal sea.'

The lines have some assonance, but what else? What are we
to say of this well-loved hymnology and of the sense it
breathes of truth as comfort and of comfort as truth?

The burden of this charge from outside the Christian faith
is that it has misread the data of experience in the interests
of consolation. Personality, it is urged, is not the vital clue
— about either us or God — which Christianity takes it to
be. A true religion, these critics insist, must of necessity be
non-consolatory. We must 'take leave of God', and, indeed,
of ourselves, in these congratulatory terms. A true religion
must refuse to cushion life's pains and stresses with illusory
vistas beyond. The personal dimension, which is where the
yearnings belong, is not finally significant. It has, in fact, to
be disengaged from all idea of its intendedness. It must
reconcile itself to its own forfeiture in death's waiting demise.
It must allow that strict arrest of time to strip it, here and
now, of all pretension to relevance. Transience is all.

At death selfhood, at least in any form we hitherto have
known, has to be surrendered. Time runs out on us, and so
does the viability of our physique. Honesty, therefore, will
not aspire to any relevance beyond 'this mortal coil.' The only
sure wisdom is to concede how altogether expendable we
are and allow that honesty to inform our reading of the
world. Whether reluctantly or indifferently, we should
consent to our cessation as centres of individual consciousness and live accordingly. We should see notions of the
beyond as inordinate extensions of illusion. Eternal life which
may delude us now will certainly elude us then.

There have been forms of this bleak philosophy capable
of great compassion — compassion, that is, in toiling to teach
mankind to be free of the illusion. But is there not, in such
compassion, more than a hint against its energising premise?
It cares — if only to disabuse of what caringness implies. It
cherishes persons on the premise of personality disqualified.
It pities, but the pity which is its spur to action is not
allowed to be the key to meaning. It will not sing with William
Blake that in 'mercy, pity, peace and love' are 'the human

form divine.' Blake's conviction was that the features that most wistfully characterise *our* being are precisely those which disclose the essentially real, the divine. This is the truth of the Incarnation as Christians hold it, the truth which, rather than denying what is most tenderly and purposefully ours, invites us to trust it as deriving from its eternal counterpart in God.

On this showing distrust can only be a sort of double-crossing of ourselves, a false anticipation of negation, an opting for despair lest we should be deceived by hope. Opting for confidence is not then, as sceptics fear, some vain will for consolatory illusion. It is a perspective for which the acceptance of meaning is no longer a concern to be consoled. Discipleship takes care of whatever is legitimate in fear. Finitude is gathered into fulfilment. 'The human form divine' discerned in God through Christ certifies 'the human form divine' which we acknowledge in ourselves, our being and our destiny and, meanwhile, our mortal consecration. This adventure is all the comfort we need.

It is this sense of things reciprocal between man and God which underlies the faith in Incarnation. To find 'God in Christ' is not some abstruse, elusive philosophy, an enigma wilfully concealed in a formula, a subtlety embarrassing a proper theism. Nor is it an idle construct arbitrarily erected on a history innocent of its meaning. Throughout in these chapters we have been studying the credentials of Christian theology with Jesus as the touchstone. Creation, nature, law, covenant, hope, Messiah — all these are the antecedents of the fulfilment. History leads us to realise what we can only call the vulnerability of God, as the shape and price of His omnipotence. It is clear, alike from the glory and the tragedy of man, that He will not have His purposes except as we, in turn, make them our own. We manifestly do not make them our own by exhortation, on demand. Our creaturehood, all experience seems to demonstrate, was not so designed. There is an evident conditioning of our true vocation on our free consent — a condition, therefore, which we must assume also of the creatorship which generously, largeheartedly, willed it so. That divine magnanimity we find present, in the terms to which it finally leads, in the Cross of Jesus, understanding

that Cross as epitomising what our wilful freedom means
to the uncoercive purposes God intends from a freedom
rightly willed. The righting of a freedom was the Messianic
task, its cost and means the love that suffers, its achievement
the reality of grace, its condition the experience of
forgiveness. We realise in the Cross, as the climax of
Incarnation, 'the human form' of the divine Lordship, 'the
divine form' of the human crisis in the moral world, the
crisis of self-awareness in sin and self-finding in love. It is
only in such terms that the Christian can hold either the
sovereignty of God or the significance of our human
personality. Otherwise both those truths, in their mutuality,
would be at best pretentious, and at worst illusory. But the
Christian ground — in Christ — on which we hold them
good and true is no make-belief, no self-persuasion. Like love,
its stands in its own recognizances. It authenticates itself in
being what it needs to be. In Christ its measures are in its
obligations, its proving is in these fulfilled.

Our personhood as human, and divine sovereignty as love,
find their corroboration in 'love of neighbour.' The Christian sense — if we may so speak — of our being precious
to ourselves is crucial to the perception of a precious
humanity everywhere and so to the compassion which 'pours
in oil and wine.' If our personhood is to be diagnosed as no
more than a wishfulness-to-mean, against the grain of
reality as such, then other existence must be wishful also.
Personhood, inauthentic anywhere, must be inauthentic
everywhere. The feasibility of society *per se* — certainly of
compassionate. society — turns on seeing our neighbour as
ourselves. If this is not true essentially it cannot be so morally.
Love of neighbour springs from the fact that 'he/she is as
you are,' which is the meaning of the words.

It is not that self-love is a model or a measure but a logic.
'The bundle of life' unifies and makes mutual. But this is
a faith which needs more ground than mere hearsay or circumstance. We are all burdened and appalled — if we are
alive at all — by the sheer masses of the human scene in the
panorama of the present and the long retrospect of history.
How dispensable, how negligible, the human individual, how
tragically expendable in the ravages of war and the incidence

of famine, plague or tidal wave. Can we be significantly precious when so readily extinguished by the callous desolations, the horrors and catastrophes of time and place, by all that cruelly abridges and cuts off the living years? And what of the discrimination between victims and survivors? Is the human relevance sustainable in Christian terms? The Buddha maybe has the wiser case.

Yet is not the daunting register of the human tragedy the other side of our trust in its worth? The personhood we know within ourselves we evaluate in the humanity without. 'He/she is as you are', being your 'neighbour', alone explains the tragic sense of life. The springs of compassion flow only from the reservoir of being. If futility is the truth for each inwardly, it is the truth of all at large. If the will to be me is not authentic in the self I am there can be no engagement of pity or of succour, or even of distress, with the selves around.

Love of neighbour, in their 'being as we are' must be the corollary of love to God, the love which through faith in creation and Incarnation reads a positive reality in every personal incidence of that cherished life I find within myself. We write off the very tragedies which have often been held to discredit that conviction unless we persist in it. For the tragic itself has no other measure.

None of us took prior decision about birth. Once enwombed however, through the trauma of nativity and beyond, our being proceeds only in the will to be, the will to relate, to desire, to engage, to belong. We have no doubt — in retrospect — the option to conclude that, so doing, we have misread ourselves and all mankind. But equally there is the option to find that state of things authentic, relevant, fraught both with crisis and with mystery, yet warranted by love, eternal love, in a way that death does not disqualify, either in anticipation or in fact. Then what is consolatory in faith and in worship will not be a crutch by which we contrive as cripples. It will be a poem by which we affirm the love we have discerned in our being what and who we are — alive, personal, mortal and divinely loved. Faith will be, as it were, the language of our amazement, the formulation of our gratitude.

Such was Christianity. Such it will continue to be. As we

saw in chapter 4, there belongs in baptism a proper No! to self, a will to 'let die' that of us and about us which falsifies in selfishness what selfhood was meant to be. But that falseness resides, not as some believe in individuation, so that our very existence is a snare from which we must be released by abnegation. On the contrary it is a selfishness which distorts what self was meant to be. Death to that self our selfhood must renounce is for the liberation of the authentic self of true vocation. Baptism is the Christian symbol of that dying/living in the personality. When literal death, by its proper mandate on mortality, says its physical No! to our existence in the here and now, the forfeiture of self involved has been spiritually familiar already in Christ's claim and meaning in our personhood. Death is 'the last enemy,' to be sure. We do not 'die before we die,' in any Buddhist sense. Yet those 'enemies before the last,' the crises of our personhood, we have already weathered through 'the grace of our Lord Jesus Christ, and the love of God, and the fellowship of the Holy Spirit.'

How apt, then, that in the New Testament those words became the formula of farewell, of farewell to one another in their meaning, of farewell to life itself on this mortal plane. They belong to all because they are the greeting of each. They are the poetry and the benediction of Christian decision, faith's invocation of the event-experience told in the New Testament.

But let us be clear, decision it remains. The critics, the sceptics, the despairers, the hesitants, may be right. They are not refuted by suppression, nor will mere argument dissuade them. The decision which took shape in mind and spirit, in privacy and community, when Christianity began is open still. The proof is only in the taking.

The State of Connecticut in that part of the U.S.A. known as 'New England' was founded by pilgrims in decision. The State motto runs: *Qui transtulit sustinet*, which may be rendered: 'Who brings you over sees you through.' The Christ takes the Christian into His — and their — Christianity.

A Few Books that Go Further

The artist, Vincent Van Gogh, wrote repeatedly that 'the finest paintings are inspired by nature but they must be painted from memory.' Borrow his words and for 'nature' read 'Jesus', retain 'memory' and for 'painting' have the New Testament. It is the literature of the great 'art' of discipleship responsive to, and responsible in, 'the Christ of God.'

Critics of art are far more voluminous that art itself, as the camp followers of genius. Books about the New Testament fill long shelves and go back long years. Even to list them makes a tome. Warren S. Kissinger, an officer of the Library of Congress, Washington, published in 1985 *The Lives of Jesus: A History and Bibliography*, Garland Publishing Inc. New York & London, pp. 230.

In such a vast literature it is well to be alert in all directions. But it is wise to cherish a few special mentors. One could well begin with: Stephen C. Neill & T. Wright: *The Interpretation of the New Testament, 1861-1986*, (new ed.) Oxford, 1988, where readers find a very competent survey and summary of major writing over those years, with critical insights into the movements of scholarship in the entire field.

Surprisingly, one omission is J.R. Seeley: *Ecce Homo: A Survey of the Life and Work of Jesus Christ*, London, 1865, a classic study of Jesus' ethics which caused a stir in its day, partly because, despite the striking choice of title, some felt it deliberately ignored Christology (a matter on which 'liberals' were held suspect). But this was not so: the book was a stirring presentation of what its author saw as Jesus' 'enthusiasm for humanity,' the strong 'expectancy' which Jesus aroused in terms of moral hope. The ring of the book was caught in the oft-quoted words: 'No heart is pure that is not passionate: no virtue is safe that is not enthusiastic.' The love of Jesus shed an eternal glory on the human race. Seeley, alas now 'out-of-print,' is worth a search.

Two mentors of our time to be cherished are C.F.D. Moule and C.H. Dodd. Of the former see: *The Birth of the New*

Testament, London 1962 3rd ed. 1982 and *The Origin of Christology,* Cambridge, 1977. Of the latter: *The Founder of Christianity,* London, 1970, and: *The Meaning of Paul for Today,* London, 1957.

There has come, happily, in the last quarter century, after long avoidance, a lively scholarship about the New Testament from Jewish sources, one example of which is Geza Vermes: *Jesus the Jew,* London, 1973, which sees Jesus as a wandering 'charismatic,' of a type familiar in the Galilee of his day. The depicting leaves the question whether a 'source' so limited could have fed the 'current' (to use a metaphor) flowing in the N.T. That involves the further, perennial question whether 'history' — to the exclusion of theology — suffices as the sphere of reckoning. Vermes explains that he writes purely as 'historian.'

Among many ventures in relating 'history' and 'theology' is Anthony Harvey's *Jesus and the Constraints of History,* London, 1982. He sees Jesus working within the first century context — Roman rule, Jewish law, time and place, healing power, and the Messianic hope, — all under the Judaic sense of the divine unity. The Jewishness of Jesus — which no intelligence will deny — need not, then, argue against what Christology came to mean, as if history could be honest about Jesus only by excluding the faith that came to be from him. Rather his whole significance remains profoundly Judaic in becoming universal. But such a view has deep implications for how Jewishness itself is understood by its participants both as an ethnic history and as a theology of covenant.

On this, see recently J.N. Sanders: *Jesus and Judaism,* 1985, alongside W.D. Davies: *Paul and Rabbinic Judaism,* London, 1948, who deals with the old — but persistent — delusion that Paul was the real 'author' of Christianity. W.D. Davies has also a notable *Invitation to the New Testament: A Guide to Its Main Witnesses,* London, 1967. Illuminating aspects of the Judaic background will be found in John Riches: *Jesus and the Transformation of Judaism,* London, 1974, and in Oscar Cullmann: *The Christology of the New Testament* (trans, from the German), London, 1959 — a study based on the titles the N.T. gives to Jesus. Bruce M. Metzger's *The New Testament: Its*

Background, Growth and Content, New York, 1965, is by a scholar
who has devoted much study to the text and its transmission.

A fascinating recent study, *Greek Rhetorical Origins of
Christian Faith,* New York, 1987, by James L. Kinneavy, argues,
with careful analysis, for the view that in the Greek terms,
pistis and *pisteuein* ('faith' and 'to believe'), there is the meaning
of 'persuasion' as employed in Greek education. 'Faith' would
then be the 'persuadedness' of the Christian — a meaning
close to ours here of 'decision' based on free conviction as
to truth. Kinneavy, however, is dealing only with the process
of coming to believe not with the content of the faith.

See also Werner Jaeger: *Early Christianity and Greek Paideia,*
Harvard, 1961, who finds a parallel of community-in-
conviction between the first Christians and the *ecclesia* or
citizen-assembly, of the Greek city.

Readers interested in the relation of the New Testament
to Islam — which is considerable in view of the Quranic
account of Jesus — may like to look at my *Jesus and the Muslim:
An Exploration,* London, 1985.

John Bowden's *Jesus: The Unanswered Questions,* London,
1988, will serve as well as any — by its penetrating mind and
a will to integrity with minimal conclusions about confidence
— for those who want to care sceptically. There are points
at which it seems positively to relish negativisms, not least
when it implies a subtle and unworthy manipulation of power
and control in those N.T. Epistles which read, to many of us,
as warm, tender and frank models of true pastoral heart-
feltness and human yearning. But who can be sure what
readers will find since how they read will be them reading.
The ultimate question for all 'unanswered questions' is that
it is only possible to ask them because of the inclusive
answer — already given — by virtue of which alone the New
Testament exists. What avails there for academic enquiry does
so only as the answer of Christian decision. May it be that
the same answer now is where all questions truly lead?

Listing, of books, in such a field is invidious and — as when
it happens to ships — is very one-sided. Diligent readers must
find — each for themselves — an even keel. Hopefully the
foregoing chapters may serve, a little, to see them righted.

Short Index and Biblical References

A

Aaron 39, 56
Abraham 36, 54, 60, 111, 117, 118, 129
— and Isaac 125
absolutes 10, 11
— denied to faith 21
acceptance of meaning 161
Acts of the Apostles 41, 87, 141
'in Adam' 89
agnosticism 25, 28, 130, 143, 159
Akedah 125
aletheia (truth) 143f
Amen 21, 43
Amos 112, 128
Anatolia 88
Andrew 82
Antioch 47, 120
Anti-Semitism 114, 146
— and 'chosenness' 116
Aramaic usage of Jesus 59, 69
Asia 96, 121
Ascension, the 14, 44, 50
Augustine of Hippo 100
authority 10, 21, 26, 44, 59, 60, 66, 158

B

baptism 26, 38, 88, 95f
— analogy of death 99, 164
— formula of 86, 87, 119
— of Jesus 67
Bar Kokhba 107, 125
Bartimaeus 85
Beatitudes, the 58, 118
Bethlehem 10, 73
birth, optionless 163
— in Judaism 54
Blake, William 160, 161

'body of Christ' 65, 134
Browning, Robert 2, 22, 39
Buber, Martin 51, 111
Buddha, the 72, 97, 163
Buddhism 7, 15, 16, 96f, 120, 158, 159
— Eightfold Path in 98
Buddhist and Christian view of the self 96f, 160f
Bultmann, Rudolf 137f
Bunyan, John 24, 145
burial of Jesus 44f
Butterfield, Herbert 17
Byzantium 21, 130

C

Calvary 62, 125
Camus, Albert 52
Canaan 95
Carthage 88
character, Christian 19, 88f, 102, 106f
'chosen people' concept, the 114f
— its tragic consequences 114f
—its invocation by others 115f
Christianoi 13, 101, 120
Christology, growth of 20, 67, 130, 131
— being 'in Christ' 89f
— of action 27, 126
— Jewish decision 124
— misguided sources of? 123f
Church, the 18, 21, 52, 63, 66, 105, 117, 122, 135, 138, 140
— mind of 20
cleansing 35, 39
Colosse 89

community, in Christ 64f, 195f
compromises, of faith 21, 146f
confessio fidei 19
consolation, desire for 160f
Constantine 141, 150
constraints against faith 145f
Corinth 89, 92
covenant, in Biblical faith 17, 33,
  54, 55, 60, 71, 75, 109, 113, 161
  — dilemma in 113f
  — Paul and 113
Crashaw, Richard 88
creation, doctrine of 17, 33, 52f,
  75, 109, 148, 161
  — man in 49
  — Messiahship and 53f
Cross, the 13, 19, 24, 34, 35, 37, 40,
  41, 42, 48, 62, 70, 75, 76, 85, 88,
  90, 93, 97, 118, 131, 132, 135,
  141, 146, 147, 151, 155, 161,
  162
  — folly of 27, 28
  — interpreted 35f
  — superscription of 89, 120
  — translated in baptism 96f,
  161f
Cyrus 57, 112

D

Damascus, road to 64
David 54, 60, 67, 73, 90, 111
  — 'son of' 108
death 99, 159, 163
  — and baptism 96f, 164
  — and dominion 46, 47
  — and personhood 158f
decision, Christian 13, 17f, 21, 23,
  43f, 66, 87, 103, 105, 137f, 150,
  153 (see also Chapter
  summaries)
dialogue 14f
  — with Buddhism on the self
  158f
diaspora, Christian 30, 70, 89f, 117,
  149
  — Jewish 107, 117, 149

Diognetus, Epistle to 148
disbelief, incentives to 146f
docetics, the 48, 126
Dodd, C.H. 7
Dostoevsky, Feodor 116
doubt, will to 11, 122f, 145f
doxa, 40
doxology 40
dying with Christ 96f, 159f

E

Easter 14, 29, 44, 146
  — premature? 146
Egypt 54, 74, 100, 120
ekpetasis (widening embrace) 118
election, of Jewry 115
  — pseudo claims to elsewhere 115, 116 (see also
  'chosenness)'
Emmaus 41, 48, 75
emptiness, of the tomb 45f
Ephesus 74, 78, 81, 85, 89, 92, 121
Epistles, the 2, 17, 19, 30, 65, 87,
  124
  — education in 19, 29, 67, 89f
  — nature of 22
  — the Pastoral 129
  — world of 77
Esau 114
ethics, Christian 29, 30, 88f, 106
  — and doctrine 101f
ethnicism, Jewish 109
Eucharist, the 26, 31, 81, 84, 100,
  155 (See also 'Last Supper')
  — pagan associations? 124
evil, issue of 28, 58f 119, 131, 151
exile 55, 57, 107
Exodus, the 39, 54, 99, 134
  — Book of 71
existentialism 138, 140
experience, disproving personhood 158f

F

fact and faith 8, 16, 138
fact and fulfilment 43, 64
fact and truth 71, 139, 142, 154

Liturgy, and language 155f
love, the great original in God 94,
 101
 — of neighbour 162f
 — that suffers 28, 46, 47, 119,
 156, 162
 — that surrenders 142
Luke 40, 41, 47, 57, 61, 73, 74, 75,
 77, 80, 83, 92, 118, 120, 121

M

Maccabees, the 28, 57, 74, 108, 150
Magnificat 57, 74, 75, 76
man, as creature 53f
Mark 77, 78, 80, 83, 120, 127
Mary 57, 74, 75, 80
Mary Magdalene 49, 50
Mashiah 7, 52
Matthew, 72, 73, 76, 80, 83
 — 'fulfilment' in 72f
 — and the Magi 74
 — 'the great commission' in
 86, 87
Mecca/Medina in Islam 149
memory in identity 54
Messiah, affirmed by Christian
 faith 64f
 — clues to, in Jesus'
 experience 60f
 — consciousness as 20, 61,
 126
 — concepts differing of 14,
 20, 33, 50, 55, 56, 119
 — belligerent 108
 — corporate 56
 — national 109
 — priestly 56
 — private 105
 — royal 55
 — 'suffering servant'
 paradigm 58f
 — credentiala of 7, 11, 18, 21,
 40, 62, 91, 137f
 — exclusivism and 91
 — link with creation 33f, 53f
 — perpetual futurism about
 51f, 111, 135

 — in redemption 34, 40, 62
 (see also 'the suffering
 servant')
 — scandal of a crucified 73
metaphor 9, 10, 27, 38, 155, 157
 — in 'ascension' 44
 — of 'the face' 39
 — of sacrifice 35f
 — of washing 38, 39
Milton, John 49
ministry, Christian 25, 26, 65, 66,
 71, 101
moralism without illusion 132
mortality 89, 164f
 — puzzle of 160
Moses 39, 60, 71, 90, 95, 129
 — and Matthew 76
Muhammad 130, 149, 153
'mystery of Christ the' 126
mystery, final 28, 155
mystic cults in gnosticism 128
myth 9, 27, 138, 139, 157
 — of Jesus? 138f
 — of Christian origins? 140f

N

Nathaniel 54, 83
nations, the 109f
 — anxiety breeders for Israel
 111
Nazareth 14, 29, 58, 66, 129
 — placarded on the Cross
 132
nationality 148f
neighbour, love 162, 163
New Testament 7, 8, 16, 18, 29f, 69f,
 88f, 133f
 — consensus in 33, 42, 69f
 — dispersion in 30, 70, 89f,
 117, 149
 — geographical partiality of
 120, 121
interplay of times in 19, 73f
 — liturgy in 22 (see also
 Magnificat)
 — pastoral nurture in 19, 88f

The following chapter synopsis may help in the location of broad inclusive themes, like 'Christ', 'Christian', 'Christianity', 'faith' and 'love' which cannot well be indexed by page or isolated from a whole.

Chapter 1: The New Testament as document, whence? p.29: a history, an education and a community via Jesus as the Christ, fulfilling ancient hope realised in a teaching, suffering personality — this realisation and its interpretation p.36f: burial and Resurrection — the warrant of truth p.44f

Chapter 2: Messiah — the Jewish principle of hope deriving from divine liability to history, rooted in creation p.51f: Judaic forms of hope p.54f: the 'servant' Jesus' clue realised as such in the experience of rejection within ministry p.57f and apprehended in, and as, the making of the Church p.64f

Chapter 3: Gospel formation reviewing and recording Messianic truth-through-personality within the context of its community life p.69f: the evangelists as authors, their instincts of mind p.74f the fourth evangelist p.78f.

Chapter 4: Christian incorporation in the Christ in the dispersion of the faith p.88f. The Gospel in the Epistles p.92f: participation as baptism and Eucharist p.96f.

Chapter 5: A universal humanness deriving from the manner of Jesus' Messiahship p.105f — ethically and spiritually demonstrated and made imperative p.109f — contrasted with Messianic privacies and the entail they incur p.116f

BIBLICAL REFERENCES

Old Testament		**Micah 4.4.**	**54**
Genesis 1.1	52, 53	Habakkuk 2.4	35
Exodus 17.16	54		
Numbers 6.24-26	39	**New Testament: The Gospels**	
Deuteronomy 6.4	124	Matthew 5.4	59
Deuteronomy 21.23	125	Matthew 5.18 et al.	43
1 Samuel 2	74	Matthew 5.27 et al.	76
1 Kings 4.25	54	Matthew 6.14	92
1 Kings 8.29	19, 89, 90	Matthew 8.20	33
2 Kings 18.31	54	Matthew 10.30	59
Psalm 4.6	39	Matthew 11.27	79, 134
Psalm 22	76	Matthew 11.28	81, 93
Psalm 33.6	102	Matthew 15.24	134
Psalm 89.15	39	Matthew 16.13-15	61
Psalm 90.8	39	Matthew 16.21-23	41
Psalm 148.5	102	Matthew 18.20	20
Isaiah 2.2	111	Matthew 19.17	133
Isaiah 2.4	111	Matthew 26.13	134
Isaiah 36.16	54	Matthew 26.29	135
Isaiah 42 to 53	35, 37	Matthew 28.6	45, 46
Isaiah 45.1	112	Matthew 28.19-20	86, 87, 119
Isaiah 53.1	57, 73	Mark 7.15	93
Isaiah 53.5	36, 37	Mark 9.40	92
Isaiah 53.6	37, 151	Mark 11.10	55
Isaiah 53.7	35	Mark 14.43	35
Isaiah 60.1-3	74	Mark 14.65	94
Hosea 11.1	74	Mark 15.47	48
Amos 5.18	55	Luke 6.23	92
Amos 6.1	143	Luke 6.28	92
Amos 9.7	112	Luke 9.35	67
Micah 4.2	111	Luke 15.1	61